The
Crewes
of
Crewe Hall

by Ray Gladden
edited by Gerry Park

About the Author

Ray Gladden was born in Crewe in 1925. Apart from service as a radio operator in the merchant navy during the second world war, he lived in the town all his life, and died there in 2010. From childhood, he knew Crewe Hall well. His uncle, Robert Spence, was head gardener at the Hall, and lived with his wife, Grace, at the Gardens Cottage. From 1948 to 1984, Ray himself worked at the Hall during its industrial phase.

The Author (left) with his uncle (centre), head gardener Robert Spence, outside the peach house at Crewe Hall in 1927.

About the Editor

Jerry Park lives in Nantwich. He is the author of *The Millers' Tale: A Victorian Fylde Family*, an account of the 19th century family that owned the great Preston cotton house of Horrockses.

About this Booklet

Ray Gladden had a life-long interest in Crewe Hall, and over many years researched the history of the Crewes and their principal home. Using the primary and secondary sources listed at the back of this booklet, he prepared a longer and more discursive text than is issued here. Unable to find a commercial publisher, shortly before his death he invited Jerry Park to reduce the material to a scale that would allow private publication at an economic cost. The opportunity has been taken to update the story, and to place some of it in a wider historical perspective. In the near future, a shorter, separate booklet on the Victorian rebuilding of Crewe Hall will be published. This will draw on research too detailed for inclusion in the present publication.

Reprinted by Nantwich Museum 2021,
Nantwich Museum, Pillory Street, Nantwich CW5 5BQ;
Telephone 01270 627104; www.nantwichmuseum.org.uk.
Nantwich Museum Trust Limited Registered Charity: No 509386

ISBN 978-0-9567789-1-8

CONTENTS

Editor's Dedication

To the memory of
my friend Ray Gladden 1925-2010
and my father Ronald Park 1913-1954

Chapter 1

ANCIENT AND MODERN

We are peers of highest station,
Paragons of legislation,
Pillars of the British nation!
Tantantara! Tzing! Boom! [1]

'Everybody loves a lord.'

The peerage remains a distinctive British institution, despite the waning powers of the House of Lords since the Parliament Act of 1911 and the removal of hereditary peers from automatic membership in 1999. Yet fallacies about the peerage in Britain verge on caricature. Popular misconceptions of a lord include a family that 'came over with the Conqueror'; an estate passed down from father to son in unbroken succession for twenty generations; a country house that is Elizabethan or, at a pinch, Georgian; and politics that have been Conservative for as long as that party has existed in some form.

The reality is more complex. Although there is no longer a Marquess of Crewe, and Crewe Hall is no longer a family home, the latest printed edition of *Burke's Peerage, Baronetage and Knightage* lists 127 other peerages under the letter C [2]. Of these, only sixteen derive from titles created before the 18th century. Forty-one of the titles - almost one third – belong to non-hereditary peers created as a result of the Life Peerages Act of 1958. Twenty-two of the hereditary peerages were created in the 19th century, and thirty-four in the 20th.

Even among long-running peerages, estates have not passed placidly from father to son. Ever since the fourth Lord Percy became the first Earl of Northumberland in the late 14th century, the Percy family has been famous in English history through the combined efforts of Shakespeare and Walter Scott. True, there is still a Duke of Northumberland at Alnwick Castle, but his surname should be the more humdrum Smithson - the Yorkshire family into which a Percy heiress married before the second dukedom of Northumberland was created.

And, if relatively few peerages demonstrate unbroken succession, even fewer illustrate unbroken success. The Dukes of Marlborough of Blenheim Palace in Oxfordshire famously produced little enduring talent between John Churchill (the great war leader of the early 18th century) and his direct descendant Winston Churchill (the great war leader of the mid 20th century). That is not to say that the Marlboroughs, or any other peers, were inactive. They might serve in the House of Commons before translation to the House of Lords, and occupy office at court, in government or in the burgeoning empire. Less ambitious, but more local, they might act as magistrates, or seek election (after 1888) to county councils. For younger sons, there was the army or navy; or holy orders in the Church of England, followed by appointment to a comfortable family living and ecclesiastical preferment both home or colonial.

The family politics of the peerage were not invariably Conservative. From the point when the Tories (Conservatives) and Whigs (Liberals) slowly took shape from the 'Court' and 'Country' parties of the late 17th century, many aristocratic families were Whigs. And although Home Rule, as a practical solution to the Irish Question, fatally split the Liberal party in 1886, some distinguished peers remained Whig - among them, the Lord Crewe of the time. Even in the 1920s, a number of hereditary peers defected to the newly-risen Labour Party, usually as a personal expression of 'internationalism' after the horrors of the first world war.

Nor are all the great houses of England of ancient origin. In his *England's Thousand Best Houses*, Simon Jenkins lists under the letter C sixty-two buildings that can be described as country houses [3]. Of these, only five are predominantly of a period before the 16th century. Of the remaining fifty-seven, ten are largely or wholly 16th century; ten are 17th century; twenty-three are 18th century; twelve are 19th century; and five are 20th century. While it might be expected that over one third of these properties would be predominantly 18th century, it is more surprising to find that over one quarter belong to the 19th century or later.

Many of these themes - the interrupted family succession and altered family name; the changing political allegiances; the relatively few 'high achievers' down the generations; the variable commitment to public life; the relatively late date of the family home - are present in the story of the Crewes of Crewe Hall. But in one respect at least their story conforms to stereotype: the history of the Hall begins with William the Conqueror.

After the Norman invasion of England in 1066, William I sent his troops to subdue a series of rebellions in the country. The Norman army vanquished the Old Saxon Kingdom of Mercia and came northwards into Cheshire. In the process, many 'manors' were laid 'waste' and the population put to flight.

Crewe Hall The south elevation engraved by Hollar c.1656

King William installed his nephew, Hugh of Avranches ('Hugh the Fat Hunter' as the name Grosvenor prosaically translates), as the Earl of Chester. Hugh exercised local control from administrative headquarters inside the Roman walls of the city. He sub-divided his lands and created barons to rule individual areas. These barons were served by knights and lesser feudal lords, who had local powers to hold courts and authorise markets and fairs. They also had responsibility for maintaining numbers of armed men to serve the Earl of Chester and the King when necessary.

The manor of Crewe was in an area called the Warmundestrou Hundred, granted by Hugh to Richard de Vernon, who let it to the existing Saxon tenant Osmaer. A taxation assessment was made for England in 1086, and the resultant details and values were published in the Domesday Books. The entry for Crewe described how *Osmaer held the land of Crewe. He paid one hide* [100 acres] *in tax and had enough land for two ploughs. He had meadowland of one and a half acres and woodland of one league* [3 miles] *and half a league wide. It was valued at ten shillings in 1066, but was valued at only five shillings in 1086 when it was found waste* [4]. This paints Norman Crewe as a primitive agricultural landscape, more woodland than farmland, on the southern fringe of the Mara and Mondrem (now Delamere) forest which stretched northwards to the Mersey.

In his *History of Cheshire*, Ormerod noted that a Norman manor house had existed near the present site of Crewe Hall in the year 1170 [5]. He listed a tentative Crewe family pedigree from Henry de Criwa in 1150 to Sir Ranulphe Crewe in 1646. Sir Ranulphe had referred in his will to the existence of Crewes of Crewe in earlier times, without citing evidence that they had been important landowners [6]. Notwithstanding these efforts, there is no proven connection between the family of Crue or de Crue and Crewe.

Nonetheless, there are records of Crues in the 14th century. In 1346, Prince Edward called for reinforcements of Cheshire archers. Of the 300 offered, 100 were to be led by Sir William Brereton of Brereton near Holmes Chapel, and among the men-at-arms in the Prince's retinue was Sir John Hyde of Hyde, who served with a Thomas de Crue and his brother. Letters of Protection, pardoning those who promised to serve their King of certain civil wrongs, were granted on 8 July 1354 to Sir Hugh Calveley for some Cheshire men crossing to Brittany on royal service. These men included William de Crue and Hugh, son of David de Crue. In 1357, Thomas de Crue of the county of Cestre petitioned the King as *the Prince's liegeman in the county of Cestre* reminding the Prince how he came to him at the Isle of Wight. Through his sergeants-at-arms, the Prince had commanded both brothers to board his ship and serve with Sir John Hyde. De Crue had received no wages for his part in the battle of Cressy, when he had succoured his wounded brother. He therefore requested a pardon for an offence of trespass.

In a record of annuities paid by the King for military services rendered, the name of William Crue appeared between October 1397 and July 1398, and he was paid 100 shillings. In the same period, several Cheshire men were recruited to serve in the King's personal army. Among them was Henry Crue, who was to serve as a Yeoman for Life at a fee of 6d per day. On 24 February 1399, King Richard II ordered all men aged between 16 and 60 to report outside the Watergate at Chester, as Cheshire archers were needed for service in Ireland. William de Crue of Sandbach was among the names granted in the Letters of Protection.

It is unlikely that the Crewes of Crewe ever went into battle wearing their own heraldic devices, but later generations registered special effects with the Royal College of Heralds to establish their place in the social hierarchy. The Crewes' heraldic device was a white lion rampant, surmounted by a crest of a lion's paw. The White Lion public houses at Barthomley and Weston took their name from this. If local gentry approved a hostelry, their coat of arms or colours could be displayed as a recommendation to passing travellers: a sort of medieval 'Les Routiers' endorsement. In the days of bear baiting, the lion's paw was often mistaken for the bear's paw that has become identified with the Crewe family, and has been widely used in Cheshire. The Crewes' insignia can be seen above the doors of local farms and houses that the family owned at various times. The white lion rampant appears on the crest of Crewe Alexandra Football Club.

From the days of Osmaer the Saxon in 1086, the site of Crewe Hall has had many occupants. The name of Criwa is both Old English and Welsh in origin, meaning a ford or crossing place. Although there were families in Norman times with similar names to Crewe, there is no evidence that they lived at Crewe. In the mid 12th century, a Henry de Criwa witnessed a deed drawn up for the third Baron of Wych-Malbank, but there is no indication where he lived. Crewe may have become corrupted to 'De Crue' in the next century, when a Thomas de Crue is mentioned in a charter witnessed by William de Wistaneston.

Thomas de Crue died in 1292. Of his three daughters, the eldest, Joan, married Richard Praers of Barthomley in 1319. Richard's father had been granted the Manor of Crewe from Randle de Merton in August 1278 when it reverted to the Earl of Chester after the Countess of Warwick died without heirs. The Manor of

Crewe formed part of the lands held by the Praers family. It continued in their ownership until it passed to the Fouleshursts when Elizabeth, daughter of Thomas Praers, married Sir Robert Fouleshurst. The Fouleshursts occupied a manor house that probably dated from the 12th century. The location of the old Fouleshurst house is shown on the early pictures of the present Crewe Hall [5]. Its structure was almost certainly defensive in part [8].

Sir Robert Fouleshurst served Lord Audley of Heighley Castle as an esquire, together with Sir John Delves of Doddington, Sir Thomas Dutton of Dutton and Sir John Hawkestone of Wrinehill. According to local legend, all four supported Lord Audley at the Battle of Poitiers in 1356 with Edward, the Black Prince. The Prince reputedly rewarded them for their bravery before they returned to Cheshire, where Robert's descendants continued to hold the Manor of Crewe for approximately two hundred years [7]. The badly wounded Lord Audley is said to have divided his subsequent military pension of 500 marks among his four esquires. Legend or not, Sir Robert was the most famous of the Fouleshursts. His fine carved effigy - he died in 1390 - in the Crewe chapel in Barthomley church reflects his prestige.

Four generations after the celebrated Sir Robert, the Fouleshursts were still serving king (by then, Henry VIII) and country when another Sir Robert Fouleshurst was killed on Flodden Field in 1513. But during the next generation, Fouleshurst influence waned. Their estates, including the Manor of Crewe, were sold in 1562 to Sir Hugh Cholmondeley. In 1579, they passed to Sir Christopher Hatton, Queen Elizabeth I's Lord Chancellor, and then to his nephew, Sir William Hatton, After Sir William's death, his widow Elizabeth married Sir Edward Coke, the Chief Justice of England, bringing £160,000 with her - an immense fortune for the time.

A colleague and friend of Coke was a signatory at the wedding. His name was Ranulphe Crewe, and the dynasty that he founded was to preside at Crewe Hall for over 300 years.

Chapter 2

KING AND PARLIAMENT

Sir Ranulphe Crewe

Sir Randle Crewe, the lord of this manor,
Was born at Nantwich, the son of a tanner.

At the beginning of the 17th century, England and Wales had an estimated population of over 4,000,000. Although over 200,000 people lived in London, the largest cities thereafter were Norwich (30,000), Bristol (20,000), York and Newcastle upon Tyne [10]. Nantwich was an important Cheshire town, but its population was probably no more than 2,000 [9]. Birmingham and Manchester were obscure villages. Crewe was scarcely on the map.

'It was possible to define men according to their social rank', but there was a surprising degree of social mobility between the upper and lower gentry, and inter-marriage between economic classes [10]. In particular, a man put any serious money he made into land, partly because there were few other investment opportunities, partly because landowners controlled taxation levels as members of parliament so made sure that land was under-taxed. This widening of the landed squirearchy was a social phenomonen of the early 17th century, and ascribed by some historians as a cause of the civil war that was to follow shortly after.

Sir Ranulphe Crewe (1558-1646), who built Crewe Hall between 1615 and 1636, belonged precisely to this class. He was born in the Nantwich house that still stands as 140 Hospital Street. Although documents variously record his forename as Randal, Randall, Randull, Randolph, Randolphe, Randulph and Randulf, Sir Ranulphe himself subsequently used this spelling in signing *with my owne proper hand* each of the five pages of his own will (see cover) [6]. His father, John Crewe, was an ambitious man known in Nantwich as 'Golden Roger'. Although the source of John Crewe's entrepreneurial wealth is unknown, he was ambitious and was said to have wanted to recover family estates and manorial rights that had been in other hands for three centuries. When he died at Nantwich in 1598, he was described as 'Gentleman'.

John and Alice (nee Mainwaring) Crewe had three sons and two daughters. Ranulphe's elder brother, Thomas, was also born in Nantwich, but lived after his

The Founder, Sir Ranulphe Crewe painted by
Sir Peter Lely

marriage at Steane, near Brackley in Northamptonshire. He pursued a legal and political career similar to Ranulphe's, and was elected Speaker of the House of Commons in 1625. He died at the age of 68, on 1 February 1633. His bequests included a sum to erect and maintain a hospital for the poor of Hospital Street in his home town. The income from this bequest (and from one similar from Ranulphe) were distributed to the poor of Hospital Street until 1733. In 1767, John Crewe diverted the funds to build and endow the Crewe Almshouses in Beam Street. In 1975, these were joined at Beam Street by the Edmund Wright Almshouses, which had been moved stone by stone from their original location near Churche's Mansion.

After giving prominent support to the Parliamentarians in the Civil War, Thomas Crewe's son, John, became Lord Crewe of Steane. His daughter, Jemima, married Edward Montague, a cousin of Samuel Pepys, who frequently mentioned *My Lord Crewe* in his diary. Lord Crewe's son Nathaniel was a *smooth and successful clergyman* who became Bishop of Durham, serving in the Upper House as both a Temporal and Spiritual Lord. The Crewes of Crewe relished these connections, to which there are several visual references at Crewe Hall. However, both the peerage of Crewe of Steane, and the baronetcy of Harpur-Crewe of Calke Abbey which descended from it through the female line, are now extinct.

To return to Ranulphe Crewe. The reigns of Edward VI and Elizabeth I saw the revival of the limited public education system that had been lost to some degree through their father's dissolution of the monasteries. It is believed that Ranulphe was educated at Nantwich Grammar School (founded 1560) and then at Shrewsbury School (founded 1552), establishments of relatively recent foundation that were benefiting the aspirant lower *bourgeoisie* much as the

Education Acts of 1918 and 1944 would do in the 20th century. He entered Parliament as the Member for Brackley in 1597, at the age of 39. Six years later, he was called to the bar.

Ranulphe married twice. In 1598, when he was 40 and a *Counsellor at Law in Lincoln's Inn*, he married Juliana Clippesby from the place and house of the same name in Norfolk. Juliana was 24, and she bore him three children: Clippesby, Juliana and John, to whom she died giving birth. While mourning a young wife, Ranulphe profited by a *fair inheritance* from the Clippesby connection [8]. Four years later, he married another Juliana, daughter of Edward Fusey of London and widow of Sir Thomas Hesketh. It is significant that Ranulphe was able to purchase the estates, fees and manorial rights of Crewe and Barthomley a year later. Nonetheless, seven more years passed before construction began in 1615 of a new mansion to replace the old Fouleshurst manor house at Crewe.

Despite this evidence of Ranulphe's growing prosperity, he was living in difficult times for those associated with government and the King's service. King James I held fixed views on the divine rights of the monarch to govern the country, and was in constant dispute with Parliament. A second Parliament was convened on 14 April 1614. At the age of 56, and now the Member for Cheshire, Ranulphe Crewe was elected Speaker of the House of Commons. His election by Parliamentary colleagues as their leader at a time of tension between King and Parliament suggests his particular qualities and strengths.

Parliament remained at odds with James I, and refused to meet his demands. Inevitably, the King blamed the Speaker, but Ranulphe Crewe riposted that ...*he could do nothing more to further the King's business without prejudicing the privileges which it was his duty to uphold*... After further wrangling, James dissolved this second Parliament.

The Second Wife Julia, wife of Sir Ranulphe Crewe, painted by Peter Lely

Given Crewe's recent royal putdown, it seems surprising that he was knighted so soon afterwards, on 8 June 1614 [11]. However, then as now, honours were sold, and anyone worth more than £40 per year could apply for a knighthood. Between 1611 and 1619, their sales raised £101,000 for the Exchequer. The boom year of 1603 saw the creation of no fewer than 934 new knights. The going rate when Crewe was knighted was just under £500. On a royal visit to Chester in 1617, the King tried to sell a knighthood to the mayor, despite the city's gift to him of one hundred gold Jacobius, plus considerable junketing at civic expense. Mr Mayor tactfully declined the offer on grounds of cost.

Sir Ranulphe was content to step out of the parliamentary limelight to his more profitable legal career. On 1 July 1614, he took the degree of Sergeant-at-Law and shortly afterwards became the King's Sergeant. August 1615 found him at Taunton Assizes giving evidence for the Crown in the case of Edmund Peacham, a West Country vicar accused of high treason. Peacham had written some unfortunate criticisms of King James I and his counsellors and life style. He was tried, tortured and condemned, but died in prison before he could be executed.

King James was a notorious persecutor of alleged witches, but in 1616 Justice Winch and Sergeant Crewe were in temporary disgrace for hanging a witch at Leicester on the false evidence of a boy. This can have been only a minor setback: in a letter written in 1628 to the Duke of Buckingham, he reflected, ...*well was it with me when I was King's Sergeant, I found profitt by it...*

Parliament next met in January 1621, but Sir Ranulphe had refused to contest a seat. In 1623, when he was 65 years of age, he was appointed Attorney General. In that office, he conducted the prosecution of the Lord High Treasurer, who was found guilty of unprecedented corruption and abuse of his office.

Two years later, on the 26th January 1625, Sir Ranulphe was appointed Lord Chief Justice of the Court of King's Bench. This was evidently a popular appointment: in his 'Lives of the Chief Justices of England', a 19th century Lord Chief Justice, Lord Campbell, recorded that ...*There never was a more laudable appointment . . . to learning and independence of mind, he added patience in hearing, evenness in temper and kindness of heart...* A much-quoted judgement by Sir Ranulphe as Lord Chief Justice arose from the contested claim to the Earldom of Oxford by two gentlemen whose names were de Vere and de Eresby. The case played to Crewe's interest in genealogy and heraldry. Delivering the judgement of the Lords, Sir Ranulphe ruled for Robert de Vere in eloquent prose that is often included in dictionaries of quotations.

After King James' death in 1625, Charles I reappointed Sir Ranulphe as Lord Chief Justice, but this appointment was short-lived. Charles' unyielding faith in the divine right of Kings was even greater than his father's, and ultimately led to conflict with Parliament, and with newly-landed gentry like the Crewes. The House of Commons refused to grant Charles the supplies he needed to wage war against France and Spain. Advised by his Council, Charles proceeded to extract loans from his wealthier subjects. Claiming that urgency prevented the King from seeking Parliament's approval, Letters of Commission were despatched on 13 October 1626 demanding that the loans be made immediately available to the Crown.

There was immediate uproar both in Parliament and in the country. In response, the Royal Commissioners for the Loan were directed to imprison those gentry refusing to comply, and to conscript the commoners of London into war service. When two judges refused to do so, the King consigned them too to prison. At this point, the Attorney General was sent to ascertain whether Lord Chief Justice Crewe would uphold this policy in terms of the law. Crewe's reaction was prompt and unambiguous: ...*by the Law of England, no tax or tollage, under whatever name or disguise, can be laid upon the people without the authority of Parliament; and that the King cannot imprison any of his subjects without a warrant specifying the offence with which they are charged*...

Equally prompt and unambiguous, Charles signed the royal writ dismissing Crewe on 10 November 1626. Sir Ranulphe felt unjustly deprived of the high office that he had held for less than two years, but in the continuing conflict between King and Parliament he prudently maintained a low profile. He lived in his house at Westminster in *a private and retired manner*, enduring loss of income as well as loss of office. In June 1628, he estimated this loss at nearly £3,000 for the period since his dismissal.

Crewe Hall had been in its eleventh year of construction when Sir Ranulphe was dismissed, and his reduced income delayed completion for a further decade until 1636. No original plans survive of this Jacobean house, nor any record of its architect or of the masons who constructed it. However, Ranulphe Crewe spent his working life in London, and moved in circles where important country houses of recent decades, such Longleat in Wiltshire, Blickling in Norfolk, and Hardwick in Derbyshire, would have been discussed. Moreover, there was a good local example of a smaller house at Dorfold in Nantwich, built for Ralph Wilbraham in 1616. Possibly John Crewe, Ranulphe's second son, supervised the later building work at Crewe: he may well have lived locally, as in 1636 he married Mary Done, a girl from a well-known family in Ukinton.

Daniel King's 'The Vale Royal of England', published at Chester in 1656, includes the engraving 'The Prospect of Crewe Hall'. This was drawn and etched by Wenceslaus Hollar (1607-1677), a skilful artist who industriously produced around 2,700 drawings of buildings during a career spanning fifty years. Despite his average output of roughly one picture per week, Hollar's detail and accuracy are undisputed, and art historians regard him highly. His picture shows the then recently completed Hall: a small, square building with tall chimneys and an open courtyard at its centre. Its front door was located as it is today, but plumb centre of a symmetrical façade.

The fabric of the Jacobean part of the present Hall has largely survived the ravages of time and a devastating fire in 1866. The small, hard, locally-made bricks of red and blue, that form the familiar lozenge pattern on the face of the building, are those laid in the 17th century. The massive sandstone blocks that encase the structure are softer than the bricks, and there is evidence of repair and replacement with stone from Hollington Quarries near Uttoxeter.

In the 17th century building, the main room called the great hall was in the position later occupied by the dining room. Beyond the great hall lay the east hall, accessing the lower part of the main staircase [13]. The first Marquess of Crewe, who could just recall the house before the fire of 1866 destroyed many of its original features, recalled that the ...*Carved Parlour was one of the most beautiful Jacobean rooms anywhere, both in proportion and in decoration, but so far as I recollect, there as elsewhere the leaded windows with oblong and diamond panes had been removed, and no change did more to spoil the character of the house as in some of the rooms at Hatfield. The reason is clear. When larger panes of glass were made the size of the windows was properly reduced, except in some of the enormously lofty rooms of the Vanburgh era when a great deal of light was needed* [12].

The rooms would have led directly from one to another, without the communicating corridors of later houses. The small internal courtyard, open to the sky, was in the position of the present marble hall. The chapel, which was consecrated by Bishop Bridgeman of Chester on 9 August 1635, the year before the building was completed, is believed to have stood in its current location.

Outside the Hall, the 'Vale Royal' illustration shows formal gardens close to the house, with high walls beyond [7]. To the south, there was a substantial arched gateway with a solid wooden door that was too narrow for a carriage to pass through, but wide enough for horses. To the south-east, there was a pond or small lake.

The high boundary walls had identical two-storey buildings at their south-east and south-west corners. Notwithstanding their appearance of fortifications or observation points, the purpose was social rather than defensive. Overlooking the formal gardens on their side elevations, they provided private rooms to which the Crewes could escape from the bustle of the main Hall and their many relatives and servants living in uncorridored confusion. Such garden pavilions were fashionable in early 17th century country houses. Their use varied according to family needs. As at Crewe, they mostly served as rooms where occasional meals could be taken in privacy, alone or with small parties of invited guests [14, 15]. Three generations later, in 1688, an inventory lists the furniture in the *'Banketting House'*.

The range of service buildings shown in a picture of 1710 is not recognisable. The only positively identifiable structure is the pigeon cote or apple house which appears to be the present building. The original pigeon cote would have been functional rather than ornamental: pigeons were reared for the table, just as fish were bred in the fish pond.

An assessment made for Hearth Tax in 1674 listed Crewe Hall as the third largest mansion in Cheshire, with 42 hearths [16]. The largest was Cholmondeley with 58, then Rock Savage with 50, and even the Delves had 31 at Doddington. The Grosvenors at Eaton were well down the batting order at that time, with only thirteen. It is likely that the 42 hearths at the Hall included those in the ancillary buildings. If so, and the original Fouleshurst hall was included, the tax burden might have been another reason for pulling down the old building and adding a servants' wing to the Jacobean house when the facade was altered around 1700. However, there is no way of proving this, as all the illustrations of Crewe Hall show its south elevation, and give no accurate indication of extension on its west side.

Crewe Hall attracted much local interest, both at the time that it was built and later. A contemporary of Sir Ranulphe's grandson described the Hall as *that stately Fabrick of the Hall of Crew, which for many years aforegoing, had dropped and fallen in much decay... which having been the possession for some Ages, of the Falshursts, men of greate Revenue in these parts, is now again made happy by the purchase of Sir Randall Crew Knight, one of King's Majesties Sergeants at Law, and one of the most Reverend and Learned Sages of the Law in these days. Who hath brought into these remote parts a modell of that excellent form of building which is now grown to a degree beyond the building of old times for loftinesse, sightlinesse and pleasant habitation, as in and near unto London, we see many in this Age of ours* [7].

The first mail coach from London to Holyhead did not replace the horseback postal service until 1784, although from 1637 a stagecoach set out from London three times each week on the four days' journey to Chester [7]. Despite a long trek along appalling roads, Sir Ranulphe frequently visited Crewe Hall during his retirement, riding across his estates with his sons, Clippesby and John, and lavishly entertaining such Cheshire friends as Sir Richard Lea of Wybunbury, Sir Randle Mainwaring of Baddeley, Sir Thomas Smith of Hough and Sir Richard Wilbraham of Woodhey.

Crewe Hall His Lordship's Room, the only room to escape the fire of 1866, photographed c. 1905

Back in London, *Honest Crewe* (as his friends knew him) stayed quietly in his Westminster house, writing occasional impassioned letters to those who might be able to influence his cause. An appeal addressed to the Duke of Buckingham in June 1628 foundered when the unpopular Duke was assassinated two months later. Undaunted, Sir Ranulphe redirected his petition to King Charles I. Crewe continued his appeals through the years that followed. As late as 1641, when Crewe was 83 years old, Mr Denzil Holles presented an application on his behalf to the Lords at the order of the Commons, requesting them to *join in representation of this good man's loss of profit from office after fourteen years, amounting to some £26,000 . . . to stand alone in the breach, to own honesty when others dare not do it, cannot be sufficiently applauded, nor sufficiently rewarded. And that did the old man do: in a time of general desertion, he preserved himself pure and untainted.* Once again, the appeal was denied.

By then, civil war in England between Royalists and Parliamentarians had become inevitable, and Charles I raised the Royalist Standard at Nottingham in August 1642. Nantwich and its locality largely supported the parliamentary cause. John Crewe, Ranulphe's second son, was among Justices of the Peace and Gentlemen who signed their allegiance to Parliament.

Chester was a Royalist stronghold, under the command in 1643 of its Governor, General Lord John Byron. The city's defences had been strengthened and the militia, already reinforced with 300 musketeers, was now supplemented by a general call-to-arms of all citizens between the ages of 16 and 60. With the arrival of reinforcements from Ireland, the Governor led Royalist troops in a series of small battles in Cheshire in December 1643. Beeston and Hawarden castles fell to the Royalists.

The Parliamentary army had used Crewe Hall in April 1643 for imprisoning Royalist soldiers and sympathisers. Garrisons of Parliamentary forces were now placed there, as well as at Doddington and Dorfold. After Parliament lost the Battle of Middlewich, with 200 killed or taken prisoner, Barthomley was sacked. A Royalist siege of Crewe Hall was raised on 27 December 1643. The Royalists lost about sixty men in the attack, but the 100 Parliamentarians under siege ran out of food and ammunition. They surrendered the next night, when it became clear that Nantwich could not relieve them in the face of substantially increased Royalist forces. For six weeks, the 120-strong Royalist garrison held Crewe Hall, under the command of a Captain Fisher. At first, their prisoners were kept in the stables, but were later locked in Betley church. Doddington and Dorfold had fallen to the Royalists with little resistance, but Nantwich remained an impregnable Parliamentarian stronghold commanded by Sir William Brereton. The combined forces of Brereton and General Sir Thomas Fairfax decisively routed Byron's Royalists at Acton on 25 January 1644, turning local events in favour of the Parliamentarians. After being granted their request for a parley, Captain Fisher and 120 men surrendered Crewe Hall in the sixth week of their Royalist occupation on 5 February 1644.

But the civil war was not yet over. Fairfax, appointed by Parliament to a separate Cheshire command, formally requisitioned Crewe Hall in March 1644. Together with his officers and 400 men, he used the Hall as his headquarters after it had been ransacked and stripped of its valuable contents. The soldiery slept on straw in the great hall and other apartments.

In the relative security of Westminster, but in common with other landed gentry, the ageing Sir Ranulphe received demands to support the Parliamentary forces. He complained to the Council of War that the large sum of £200 to £300 was more than that asked of his country neighbours. Writing to the King's Agent, Sir Richard Browne, on 10 April 1644, he bemoaned the state of the country and the seeming inevitability of further civil conflict: *...I mourn and groan to think of it. God for his mercy's sake, look upon our miseries. If you saw the counties - how devastated, how impoverished, how defaced, it would grieve you. It is well it is out of your eye, howbeit it is familiar to your ear . . . I myself receive nothing of* *my revenue and have been plundered to a great value; the little that my son hath for him and his son is so impaired, that it will in no wise maintain them, and I protest I know not how to supply but upon credit the means of my subsisting and I hope my credit shall not fail.*

Crewe's reference to lost income was probably no exaggeration. The rents from his farms would have been unpaid due to labour shortages and the seizure or destruction of crops during the bitter local struggles. At this time, Sir Ranulphe was providing ten soldiers and two horsemen *bravely furnished,* and continued to do so until he died.

The lengthy and detailed will that he wrote and signed on 22 October 1645 throws as much light on his times as on his personal affairs. He began the five large manuscript parchment sheets with a fervent prayer to the Almighty for the care of his soul, and directed that he should be buried in the presence of his tenants at Barthomley church, where he had already built the small enclosed Crewe chapel at the east end of the south aisle to house his tomb.

His main concerns were to preserve his property intact for his male heirs, and to ensure that they were well-educated and made profitable marriages. He left most of his estate to his eldest son Clippesby; and a substantial sum to his second son, John. His law books went to his grandson Ranulphe. Finally, with half an eye on heaven, Ranulphe directed his heirs to appoint a resident parson at Crewe Hall with full board, a horse, and a salary of £20.0s.0d. a year. The duties of *...this honest and religious minister...to instruct the family in the ffeare of god...* [6].

It is a paradox that Sir Ranulphe - the builder of Crewe Hall, and the first Crewe to live there - died at Westminster. Thomas Malbon, Gentleman, Steward of the Court Baron of Crewe and churchwarden at Nantwich, summarised the death thus: *Sir Randull Crewe, Knight, A great Councellor which had byn Lord Cheefe Justice of the Kings Bench, a Religious good man and ferme for the parliament and a man of fayre possessions bothe in Cheshire and many other places . . . Departed this life at his house in Westminster the 13th day of January 1646 Beinge then of the Age of ffourscore and eight yeares or thereabouts: And* [probably following the traditional disembowelling, embalmment, and transfer to the lead coffin that both the season and the travelling distance made essential] *afterwards his bodie was brought downe into Cheshire and entombed at Barthomley whereof he was a patron in a fayre vaulte which he had made the fyfte of June 1646 at about Seyven a Clocke in thafter noone beinge ffrydaye without either Sermon or any Solemnitie ...* [9].

Thus Sir Ranulphe was duly laid to rest. The founder of the Crewes' solid prosperity was gone.

Chapter 3

LADIES AND GENTLEMEN

On Sir Ranulphe Crewe's death, his eldest son Clippesby (1599-1649) inherited the estate but died only three years later. It then passed to Clippesby's eldest son, John (1626-1684). Both Clippesby and his son were buried in Westminster Abbey, which suggests that their lives had centred on London not Cheshire. In his diary entry for 20th February 1648, the equally metropolitan John Evelyn referred to *...Sir Clippesby Crewe's fine Indian hangings and a very good chimney-piece of water colours by Breugel, which I bought for him....*

Crewe Hall A painting of the south elevation c. 1710

When John Crewe died in 1684, the Crewe estates passed to his daughter, Ann (1649-1711). Ann Crewe's judiciously arranged marriage to John Offley in 1679 had been a significant family event. The Offleys were important Staffordshire land-owners. Sir Thomas Offley, a wealthy cloth merchant from Stafford and Lord Mayor of London in 1556, had established the family at Madeley Manor, south west of the village. Five successive generations of Offleys had been lords of this manor of 3,000 acres during the 16th and 17th centuries. Izaak Walton dedicated the first edition of the 'Compleat Angler' to his friend John Offley in 1653 [17]. The union of Crewe and Offley effectively doubled the wealth of the Crewes, combining the two large landed estates of Crewe and Madeley, ultimately under the Crewe name, and raising it to the wealthiest class of country gentry. The Madeley estate was to remain in the Crewes' hands until 1921.

John Crewe-Offley - as he became on marrying Ann Crewe - took over affairs at Crewe Hall. He evidently found a sub-standard water supply. In 1685, through his steward, John Acton of Haslington, he commissioned Gabriel Smith of Knolend (now Knowl End near Barthomley) to build ...*a Waterworke, Water Tower and Water Engine to conveye and carry water*... to the Hall from a new dam on Crowbrook. Gabriel Smith is described as a carpenter, but he was clearly a water engineer as well. John Crewe supplied the timber, the ironwork, the *cisterne, brass and clay* used for installing the system, and the brick building to house the waterworks. He also provided all necessary labour for foundations and groundwork for the two new floodgates for *pounding up the water*, and for the digging, trenching, and laying down of pipes.

Gabriel Smith undertook to start work within three months of signing the agreement on 7 January 1688. The agreed sum for Smith's expertise and services was £23.0s.0d, of which half would be payable when he had finished the dam and floodgates, and half when he had *ffinished and completed* the full project. Additionally, Smith was to provide annual maintenance for the sum of £1.0s.0d., payable in half-yearly instalments at Lady Day (25 March) and Michaelmas (29 September) [18].

John Crewe-Offley died in 1688, the inventory and valuation made of his *goods, cattells and chattels* illustrated the life-style and furnishings of Crewe Hall in the late 17th century [19]. The standard of furnishing seems frugal, but was probably typical of a gentleman's household of the time. Sir John's personal items are interesting to note: *Wearing apparel £2 0s.0d.; Nappery and Lynen £10 0s.0d.; One pair Gold Shoe Buckles £5 0s.0d.; Ready money in his Purse £14 5s.0d.; Broad Gold in his Purse (84 peeces) £96 12s.0d.; Gold Watch £8 0s.0d.; Plate of all sorts £389 0s.0d.; Goods unpraised £5 0s.0d.; Mower* [more] *in his purse Eleven Ginneys £11 16s.6d.*

This inventory was taken at the Hall on 2 October 1688 - the start of winter, during which some of the livestock would be consumed. It began with the household livestock, which included ten milking cows, 13 other cattle, 29 sheep and 16 swine. Nineteen horses were kept at Crewe Hall, including four saddle horses valued at £20.0s.0d; five carthorses, £8.0s.0d; and one 'market mare', £1.10s.0d.

Contents of the barns included hay at £30.0s.0d; *Corne* at £18.0s.0d; 66 cheeses in the storehouse at £3.0s.0d.; *Turves and Coales* £10.0s.0d, Peas £2.0s.0d, Oats £1.4s.0d. and Rye 8s.0d. The March Beer Cellar held 2 hogsheads of *buttery beer*, four hogsheads of ale, two hogsheads of March beer and a part hogshead and 12 bottles of white wine. In a *small beer cellar* were four hogsheads of small beer, and in the brewhouse 31 empty hogsheads. In the ale cellar were wine and mead, along with three hogsheads of ale. The contents of the cellars had a value of £34.16s.6d, but of equal value at £36.16s.8d. were *230 measures of Mault.*

In the kitchen, there were eight sides of bacon and *one mouton*, which with furniture totalled £3.14s.0d. The kitchen brasses, £2.0s.0d, and iron ware, £1.0s.0d, were clearly worth less to them than the pewter ware, which was valued at £47.0s.0d.

The son of John and Ann Crewe-Offley, a second John (1681-1749), formally shortened his surname to 'Crewe' by an Act of Parliament of 1708. The Whig MP for Cheshire from 1705 to 1710, he married Sarah Price, daughter of Morgan Price of Nantgwared, Breconshire and had two children: John and Randulph.

The Offleys' manor house at Madeley, dating from 1556, was pulled down in 1749, when it was said to be worth £20,000 [8]. It is possible that the decision to reside at Crewe rather than Madeley had been taken before the end of the previous century. The image of Crewe Hall painted around 1710 is significantly different to that depicted by Hollar around 1655 [20]. The original oriel windows had been replaced with the full height bays that exist today; more elaborate shaped gables had been added, with balustrades above; the construction of chimneys had been changed; and a grand cartouche had been inserted over the main front doorway. Funded from the fruits of the union of the Crewe and Offley families, these alterations were undertaken around 1700. However, substantial change to the chimney construction and configuration suggest there had been earlier improvements to the accommodation, and John Crewe-Offley's inventory of 1688 refers to a *chamber next the Great Dining Room*, indicating that corridors connecting the rooms may already have been constructed. In any event, Crewe Hall chapel was used on 19 August 1701 for the marriage of John Crewe-Offley's sister, Mary, to Robert, seventh Viscount Kilmorey.

John and Sarah Crewe's elder son, John, was returned as a Tory Member of Parliament in 1734. He did not endear himself to all of his Nantwich neighbours by lavishing the customary hospitality on the local electorate to secure its votes. On 14 January 1734, William Maisterson, Justice of the Peace at Nantwich, wrote to the Whig MP, Sir Robert Cotton, objecting that the Crewes spared ...*no Pains, nor any Expence, to influence the inferior Voters in this Town...*, and protested that John Crewe for several months past ...*had allowed constant refreshment and given unlimited orders for the spiriting up their Dependants.* Alongside Lord Cholmondeley's son Charles, John Crewe was re-elected unopposed as MP for Cheshire in 1741 and 1747 [21].

Crewe Hall from an engraving c.1742

John and Sarah Crewe's younger son, Randulph, was Rector of Barthomley from 1758 to 1777, and married Ann Read. Their descendants were the Crewe-Read family of Llandinam, near Welshpool in Powys.

Inevitably, the Crewes were influential in Cheshire affairs. Through their ownership of the manors of Barthomley, Crewe and Sandbach, they could largely control taxation, church appointments, property rents, and many lesser matters such as the appointment of the parson and the town bellman at Nantwich. As the 1762 proceedings of the Court Baron of Crewe demonstrate, the local rules made by the citizens of the town could be effectively asserted through the Crewes as owners of the manor. Grant of a tenancy sometimes depended on attendance at this Court: James Smith, a small Crewe tenement holder, had to pay annual rent of £1.6s.8d; supply two capons at Easter, or put in five days teamwork a year; and attend the Court when it met.

A typical 36-acre farm at Hale was rented to Robert Perkin for £45.6s.0d. yearly, plus one shilling for the Steward's Annual Dinner. The Crewes retained all mineral and hunting rights over the land. Perkin was required to perform two days' teamwork a year, and had to accept the usual conditions of repairs to buildings, and maintenance of hedges and ditches. He could not sell his manure because he was required to spread it all on his own farm. In common with other landlords, the Crewes strictly controlled the way their tenants used their land, to

Conversation Piece The Crewes painted in the drawing room at Crewe Hall c. 1743 by Arthur Devis. Left to right: John Crewe (1707-1752); his mother, Sarah Crewe (nee Price); his brother Dr Joseph Crewe, rector of Barthomley 1739-58 and Astbury 1758-82; his son John Crewe (child with stick), later first Baron Crewe; John Crewe-Offley (1681-1749); unidentified; Elizabeth Crewe (nee Shuttleworth); unidentified young lady; Dr Randulph Crewe, rector of Barthomley and Warmingham 1758-77; unidentified; Sarah Crewe; Charles Crewe.

ensure that it was *well marled and not over-cropped* [23]. Marl was clay that contained calcium carbonate, potash and phosphoric acid. Dug out and spread over the land, it improved cropping for up to twelve years before it needed renewal. This was adopted from the 13th century until about 1840, when lime, milled bones and other methods replaced it. About 1790, the war with France inflated food prices, and stimulated much digging of marl. The resulting 'pits', as they are called in Cheshire, filled with water, but one survives alongside Weston Road.

Rents were payable twice yearly, at Lady Day and Michaelmas. Landowners generally granted leases for the lives of the tenant, and that of his wife and brothers, at rents lower than their proper valuations. By levying a heriot on a new tenant entering into a fresh lease, landowners obtained cash advances, but at the expense of reducing future rents.

Despite these known details, the recorded activities of the two generations that followed the elder John Crewe-Offley are sparse. Given that his son and grandson both represented Cheshire in several Parliaments, this is surprising. However, it may be that muniments were destroyed in a major fire at Crewe Hall in 1866, or (as the Marquess of Crewe believed in the 20th century) that the family were too busy with their day-to-day lives as country gentry to develop the habit of keeping records.

One of the few records of the Crewes during the mid 18th century is a letter that the steward William Rawlins wrote on 3 April 1724 to Sarah Crewe in London: *If my lady wants any money to pay of your bills before you leave the town be pleased to let me know that I may have the opportunity to send same up by a safe waggon. I have sold two of the bullocks according to her ladyship's orders for £16.5.0. I have marked all the old decayed trees for cordwood in the Desmesne lands and other hereditaments about Crewe and I hope to sell the bark at a very good rate* [presumably to Nantwich leather tanners]. *I should be glad to hear that all of you are in good health with all humble duty and service, your most obedient servant* [22].

Yet despite the humdrum nature of the few available records, it is clear that Sir Ranulphe's descendants were managing their inheritances competently if not with any particular panache. The next generation of Crewes would supply the panache - but at a price.

Chapter 4

TRUE AND BLUE (AND MRS CREWE)

The First Baron Crewe

John Crewe (1742-1829) was the elder son of John Crewe MP and Ann Shuttleworth, He had a younger brother, Richard, and three sisters: Elizabeth, who married John Hinchliffe, a future Bishop of Peterborough; Sarah, who married Obadiah Lane, vicar of Longton in Staffordshire; and Frances, who married General Watson.

Celebrity (I) The first Baron Crewe painted as a young man by Pompeo Girolamo Batoni.

John was only ten years old when his father died in 1752, but did not inherit the family fortune until he came of age in 1763. After attending Westminster School and Trinity College, Cambridge, he completed his education on the almost obligatory Grand Tour. He travelled through Europe with his tutor and future brother-in-law, Dr John Hinchliffe. In Rome, the Italian artist, Pompeo Batoni, painted him; and in Venice he bought a sketch from Canaletto of the Campanile and a view of Whitehall. He also acquired a *...not very large collection of Dutch and Italian pictures some of them of considerable merit...*[12].

His 'coming of age' party was held at Crewe Hall for 4,000 relatives, friends, servants and estate workers - not then an exceptional number of guests for the head of one of Cheshire's most important families. As Henry Holland was to write in 1808, *there are few counties of equal extent with Cheshire in which the numbers of landowners seem so considerable*[22].

John Crewe had real money. He was one of fifty noblemen in Cheshire whose annual income exceeded £3,000, and his annual earnings of £10,000 made him one of the wealthiest and most eligible young men in London Society. On his return to London from Europe, he took a house in Grosvenor Square next door to that of the Prime Minister, the Marquess of Rockingham. In 1764, he was elected a member of the Society of Dilettante; and in the same year was appointed Sheriff of Cheshire while still only twenty-three years of age. The following year, he entered Parliament as the Member for Stafford.

In 1766, he married twenty-two-year-old Frances Ann Greville at St George's, Hanover Square. His bride was already a Society beauty, having been twice painted at the age of sixteen by Sir Joshua Reynolds; and she sat for him again after her marriage. Although Reynolds was said to have rated her beauty higher than her brains, she patently had immense charm and personality, and could more than hold her own in the literary and political circles in which the young couple began to move.

Michael Allen (the author of a study of the connections between the Crewes and Charles Dickens), described Frances Crewe's ...*irresistible charm that bound people to her. She had a spice of devilry in her character, a bohemian dash of unconventionality and a quick wit. She was daring and flirtatious with men, encouraging admirers, not always discreetly. But despite her daring she wore a look of baptismal innocence. She warmed the hearts of friends and acquaintances, and won their unhesitating appreciation. And though her position in society was one of high standing, her character made her, nevertheless, the good-hearted friend rather than the grand lady. Mrs Crewe was one of the most successful society hostesses of the day, firstly at Grosvenor Square, then at a house just around the corner in Grosvenor Street. It was part of the routine of a hostess to hold a regular 'salon', where good conversation could be listened to, and participated in: the success of a salon was judged by the eminence of the people attracted to it. To the home of the Crewes flocked all members of the 'ton': politicians, writers, artists, and musicians* [24].

The lives of John and Frances Crewe followed the Society calendar. They spent their winters at Crewe - John was a keen horseman and a founder member of the Tarporley Hunt, keeping some fine hunters at the Hall - and their summers in London. In between, they gathered with friends in English and Continental spa resorts, although foreign travel must have been limited by the wars that Britain was fighting at some point in every decade of John Crewe's long life except the last. Frances wrote regularly to her mother (a talented writer and poet in her own right) and to her many friends, and she kept a journal of her travels. Her letters reflect the affectionate esteem of friends like Edmund Burke and William Windham, who were frequent guests at Crewe Hall. Other friends included Richard Brinsley Sheridan who dedicated his play 'The School for Scandal' to Frances, with whom he mildly flirted. Her visitors to the Hall were invited to pen their poetic thoughts in her special book, and contributors included the politician

Celebrity (II) The wife of the first Baron Crewe painted by Thomas Gainsborough.

George Canning, and Charles Burney, Fellow of the Royal Society, music historian and father of the author, Fanny Burney.

Expeditions were sometimes made to the theatre at Newcastle-under-Lyme, which enjoyed much provincial celebrity. As a guest at Crewe, George Canning once refused to explain why he would not join such a party. Pressed by Frances Crewe, he admitted that he was unwilling to go because his mother had a role in the play they were going to see. This must have been between 1796 and 1801 while Canning was Under-Secretary for Foreign Affairs, as his mother finally quit the stage in the latter year [12]. In her 'Life of Emma Darwin', Sarah Wedgwood described a garden party at Crewe for about 100 guests, apparently in 1807. Bad weather confined the entertainment to the house, and despite luncheon at 3.00pm, followed by music and dancing, the party evidently flopped.

As the Member for Cheshire from 1768 to 1802, John Crewe was famous for 'Crewe's Act' of 1782. This disenfranchised voters in customs, excise and post office employment, and diminished ...*the influence of the Crown upon which* [their]... *positions and income* depended. His work on the repeal of duty on salt endeared him to farmers and cheese-makers in Cheshire. This tax reached £30.0s.0d. per ton during the repeated wars with France, but it was progressively reduced and finally abolished in 1825.

As popular socialites and enthusiastic Whigs, John and Frances made a greater impression on London Society and politics than all the Crewes of Crewe who had gone before them. Frances's letters indicate that John was very free with his money. He gave annual financial support of £1,200 to his particular friend, Charles James Fox, in the latter's early days as leader of the Whig party. At one of the famous Crewe dinner parties, the Prince Regent gave a toast *True and blue and Mrs Crewe!* To which Frances jauntily responded *Buff and blue, and all of you!*

George Montagu described a visit to Crewe Hall in a letter to Horace Walpole in August 1763: ...*The country is flat, sandy, poor and viewless about it, but as*

25

[John Crewe] *has a vast command and is young, he may plant and have a forest instead of a park all round him for miles...*' He sniffily noted that Crewe Hall had very few reception rooms and bedchambers, and that the Crewes were considering gutting the place to create more rooms [25]. Progress was evidently made, as Sir Grimston Harbottle rode over to the Hall from Nantwich on 21 October 1768 and reported that the drawing room had been modernised and hung with paper and good paintings, including those by Sir Joshua Reynolds of Mrs Crewe, Mrs Hinchliffe with Miss Crewe, and Dr Hinchliffe, as well as four portraits by Lely. *There seems to have been a great many servants and horses; a hall porter occupied a great chair in the hall, which seems superfluous in what was then a remote rural district. There was always a French cook and one of the numbers was Grillion, who afterwards kept a well-known London hotel, where the Club that made his name famous held its first meeting in 1812* [12].

The landscaping and planting of the park, together with the alterations to the Hall, became a priority for John Crewe when he embarked on his socio-political career. Around 1780, he and Frances substantially altered Crewe Hall, improving the principal interiors, and adding a large and expensive service wing to the west side that projected beyond the original south side. Neale's 'Views of Seats' (1818) illustrated this additional west wing, a modest extension with additional reception rooms and bedrooms [26]. The size and shape of this extension can be visualised by standing to the south of the front door, and imagining the existing west wing extension as a smaller symmetrical block, with a central bay window, but only about half the height of the main building. Other refurbishments recorded between 1772 and 1804 included bedroom alterations, and the painting of doors, windows, shutters and chimneypiece in *dead white.* Work in February 1783 included *making 16 recesses* on one side of the wine cellar and numbering and writing the *names of the Wine in white lead and Victoria black oval ground.* An estimate of £865 from J Cheney for construction of an attic storey with seven bedrooms, two storerooms, two closets and a new staircase is dated 5 August 1796. W Coomer rendered an account for £1,188.15.1½d on 3 November 1804 for building an additional storey over the kitchen and servants' hall. But some capital was available from land sales at Tattenhall, Huxley and Burwardsley that netted Lord Crewe £40,137.19s.10d. in 1802 [27].

Following the fashion of the late 18th century, the formal walled gardens of the Jacobean house were replaced with a more picturesque and open landscape that 'set off' the house to greater advantage. It is unclear whether these particular alterations were the work of William Emes (1729-1803), the celebrated landscape gardener who certainly supervised work at Crewe Hall from 1768 to 1771 [28]. Grimston Harbottle reported that *...the situation is flat and has been without a* *park. Mr. Crewe is laying one out under the direction of Mr. Eames [sic] ...the edifice is a square of a very old date and has been in its day very superb. I think it is more to be admired now for its antiquity than elegance or conveniency....* In his *Tour* of 1768, Lord Verulam mentioned that William Eames was working at Chirk and Crewe, and has been quoted as saying that the latter park *has been admirably laid out by Mr Brown* in 1747 [29]. However, his remark clearly referred to Trentham, and there is no evidence that 'Capability' Brown ever worked at Crewe Hall.

About 600 acres of open parkland, woodlands and lake surrounded the Hall. The park of 1801 comprised fifty acres of lake and 'new river', sixteen acres of

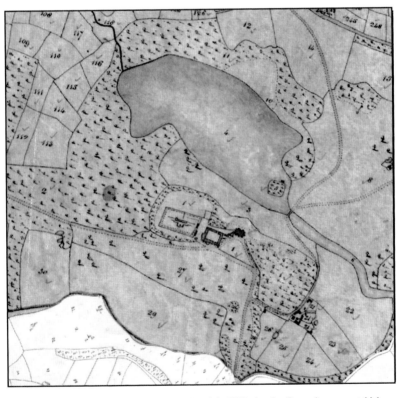

Gentleman's Residence Part of the Crewe Hall park in 1840, showing Repton's ornamental lake.

Crewe Hall An engraving of the south elevation by JP Neale published in 1822.

'pleasure gardens', three acres of kitchen gardens and hothouses inside the walled garden, three acres of orchards, an ice house, brick kiln fields and 161 acres of exclusive tree plantations [30]. Humphry Repton was employed as landscape gardener in 1791. He had taken up landscaping in about 1788 when, as a talented artist, he learned that effective presentation of his proposals was critical. In a series of watercolour sketches, he would collect his detailed schemes in a 'Red Book' to tempt wealthy clients. In Cheshire, he produced and supervised schemes for Wilbraham Bootle at Rode Hall (1790), and William Egerton MP at Tatton Park (1792). At Crewe Hall, Repton's scheme for a larger lake and new approach drives was adopted. Although no plans remain of the routes that these drives took, it is known that in 1767 there were two main approach routes. One was along the line of the drive to what was then called the Nantwich (later the Crewe Gates) lodge; and the other lay past Crewe Hall Farm to the Barthomley road [31].

While staying at Crewe Hall in May 1791, Repton penned some lines in Mrs. Crewe's album: *Thus it happens at Crewe, where, tho' Taste overflows,/ One Repton's called in to display what he knows.* (Repton published this verse in his own comedy 'Odd Whims'. Wisely, he didn't give up his day job on the strength of it.) On the same occasion, Frances Crewe recorded the comments of their septuagenarian friend, Edmund Burke, whose own 'Essay on the Sublime and the Beautiful' had influenced landscape aesthetics thirty years earlier. Regrettably, neither the 'Red Book' of landscaping proposals for Crewe, nor Mrs Crewe's album, has survived.

These improvements to Hall and grounds certainly impressed the Crewes' Society friends. When Edmund Burke made his first visit to Crewe Hall on 20 September 1788, he wrote of the long gallery *...I am vastly pleased with this place. We build no such houses in our time...*'. Richard Burke Senior described it as *...an exquisite room, that pleases me more than any I ever saw. Forty people might inhabit it, in sets or tête à têtes, or singly, with all ease and convenience. It had the effect on me yesterday of putting me quite at home in an instant....*[32].

In letters to her mother, Frances recorded that she had not visited Crewe between 1774 and 1781 but was now determined to return there often. The Crewes started to use the Hall for lavish house parties of Opposition leaders, and by 1800 it was a seat famous for its hospitality. For his services to the political life of the nation, John Crewe was created first Baron Crewe of Crewe in 1806. This was on the initiative of his long-standing friend, Charles Fox, who never climbed the greasy pole to Downing Street but was a leading Government figure.

Crewe Hall An engraving of c. 1818 of the lake and north elevation.

29

Among the servants who helped the Crewes to scale the heights of hospitality were their butler and housekeeper William and Elizabeth Dickens. William died in 1785 leaving Elizabeth with a two-month-old baby son, John. As his mother remained at Crewe as housekeeper, John Dickens spent the first nineteen years of his life with the Crewes, and the family played an important part in his upbringing. This association was an important influence on the creative imagination of John's son, the novelist Charles Dickens (1812-1870).

But John Crewe's capital projects and lavish life-style strained his finances. So did the support that he gave at various times to his own family, some of whom must have come to seem like hangers on. In particular, there was his son, the future second Baron Crewe, whom one descendant conservatively described as *extravagant*. In due course, John Crewe took over responsibility for his son's children. He also supported his own brother, Richard, seven years his junior, and married to Milborough Alpress in Kingston, Jamaica. Richard entered military service; was a major in the war against the American colonies; and rose to be a major-general. In middle age, he impressed an acquaintance at Bath as *...a clever sagacious Man of the World, a professed Gambler, living by his Profession...knowing all things and everybody, a Man of Parts, well practised in Life, prompt, intrepid and gentlemanly....*[and was]*....now supporting Himself in splendour by the Pharaoh Table which he has a share of at Brooks...*[33]. General Crewe was much loved by his family and by the brother who bankrolled him.

John Crewe also granted a lucrative church living to one of General Crewe's four sons, the Reverend Willoughby Crewe, who was a cheerful and popular parson with tastes less clerical than sporting. *He had a curate at £100 a year in each of his two livings, and from time to time, rode over to one church or the other to preach the sermon. He was fond of sport, and often went over to Madeley in search of woodcocks, with a pocket full of half-crowns for farm labourers collected to beat. He also had a pack of harriers here; and at stated intervals made an expedition to Paris for a spell of gambling. a delight even then forbidden to his cloth on this side of the Channel...*And there was Brooke Greville, on whom Lord Crewe settled an annuity of £400, afterwards raised to £800. *He was the son of Lady Crewe's brother...and...was treated quite as a son of the house at Crewe, and the Boat Room, the irregularly shaped room in the nursery wing, was set apart for his use. ...So far as I know he never had any profession but that of a 'man about town' and he developed a skill at whist which was believed to be worth £2,000 a year to him* [12].

The Crewes' money troubles steadily mounted. During 1799, Frances Crewe explained to her father-figure Dr Burney, that their considerable financial difficulties were not due to her own extravagance. She said that she had received only £200 a year as 'pin-money' until 16 years earlier, when it had been increased to £300 a year. She had never been a farthing in debt and had always 'managed', but had been embarrassed when calls were made upon her. She explained that their receipts from rents were £12,600 a year. From this they paid £5,500 in interest on debts and £1,350 on annuities. *What remains to be spent? . . .If you ask who and what can have raised this enormous debt, I can only say I don't know for certain all, but some I know are Dick Crewe, Charles Fox, late Lord Coleraine, late Lord Foley and several more Brooks' and other Companions and what has made it so very heavy is, that Mr Crewe never could sell an Inch of Land since he suffered himself to be security for all Charles Fox's debts and only what they call Judgements on all his property prevent him from power to part with a foot of Land.* Nothing had been sold, but money had been taken up at increasing rates of interest, *...since poor foolish John* [their son] *got into his scrapes...and to shew what Laxity of Morals are in this house....* Her husband would not discuss these matters with her, so her account may not be wholly reliable.

John Crewe had also lost an immense sum to Martindale, the keeper of a public gaming table. This was money that John's sister had left to accumulate in the bank for him. Martindale was fined £200 on 18 March 1797 for keeping the faro table at Lady Buckinghamshire's. Later, he was refused a licence for a new club of which the Prince of Wales was to be the patron. Frances Crewe said that *...Martindale has turned out like the rest of them and cheated them all and left them with his bond which is good for nothing...Crewe is so genteel as to say he never could suspect so fine a fellow....* In other correspondence with her sister-in-law, Sarah Lane, Frances revealed that Martindale had cost Crewe more than £3,000.

Lord Crewe's own flamboyance, the demands of his friends and family, and propitiation of his creditors finally forced him to sell land on his Cheshire and Staffordshire estates to the value of £300,000. The lost domains included land acquired through the Offleys at Darlaston near Wednesbury, which later became even more valuable as a developing industrial area [34].

Against this financial crisis, Lord Crewe's earlier social and political triumphs inevitably faded. He died in 1829 at the age of 86, having directed that each labourer on the Crewe estate should follow his cortege to Barthomley parish church. Each was also to receive £1.1s.0d. and a suit of blue clothes for the occasion - a handsome level of gratuity when field workers' day rates for weeding turnips or turning hay ranged from 1s.0d. to 1s.6d. per day, rising to 2s.0d. for harvest work with its longer hours [23].

Otherwise, by his own wish he was buried with as little expense as possible, stipulating *that neither coach nor carriage* should be in attendance [35]. It was the funeral of a disillusioned man.

Chapter 5

BROTHER AND SISTER

The Second Baron Crewe

The first Lord and Lady Crewe had four children: John, Richard, Frances (who died young), and Elizabeth Emma.

Infant Prodigy The second Baron Crewe painted c. 1775 as a child as Henry VIII, by Sir Joshua Reynolds.

Their son John, the second Baron Crewe (1772-1835), achieved celebrity at second hand through being painted in the costume of Henry VIII by his mother's friend Sir Joshua Reynolds. He was a high-spirited young man, and entered the army, serving at one time in Peking as a lieutenant on the staff of his mother's cousin, George, first Earl Macartney, who was Britain's first ambassador to China. But John also had an irresponsible streak, and at one stage ran up substantial gambling debts. After his father had raised the necessary funds to pay them off, John gave the money to an army friend in difficulties, who promptly used it to pay off the debts of yet another 'friend'.

In 1807, he married Henrietta Maria Walker-Hungerford, ...*a very attractive 35 year-old, judging from a miniature at Crewe, which is the only portrait known to exist....* She was also heiress to a considerable fortune, that had come down to her family through enterprising Scottish forebears who had developed substantial sugar plantations in Barbados. The Hungerfords lived at a manor house (since demolished) at Studley near Calne in Wiltshire, and had a town house in Cavendish Square in London.

But with Scots canniness, Henrietta Crewe's fortune had been strictly tied up. Perhaps for that reason, the marriage was unhappy and not improved by the news that John had gone through another (bigamous) wedding ceremony conducted by a disguised billiard-marker in the chapel at Crewe Hall [34]. The result of this love-match was a daughter who was brought up with the Crewe family and, according to hearsay, went on to marry the illegitimate son of John's mother, Frances Crewe. Not surprisingly, this claim has been disputed, and perhaps any illegitimate son was that of the first Lord Crewe, rather than that of his wife.

The full excesses of John Crewe have never come to light, probably because his family strenuously concealed his indiscretions. The most interesting-sounding of the family letters have been removed from the Cheshire Record Office collection of Crewe Papers. There remains the reference in his mother's letter to Dr Burney to ...*poor foolish John* [and] *his scrape'* [32]. But years later, one of John Crewe's daughters told her nephew the first Marquess of Crewe that her father had calculated that his total liabilities never exceeded £80,000. Modest by today's standards, such a level of debt was vast in its time. Taken with his parents' extravagant standard of living, this had forced the land sales that raised £300,000.

John and Henrietta Crewe produced one son, Hungerford, and two daughters, Annabel and Henrietta. When their mother died in 1820, aged 48, all three children were made wards of Chancery and came to live with their grandfather at Crewe Hall. *They inhabited the 18th Century wing at Crewe, of which the main passage then consisted of five rooms, the Valets Room at the head of the stairs, next to it the Red Room, then the Boat Room and the South and North Rooms with windows matching their respective names at the end of the passage. What is now the Chinese Room was the old schoolroom* [12].

Their grandfather, the first Baron Crewe, died in 1829. Despite the land sales, a vast estate remained, of which the Cheshire portion amounted to nearly 8,000 acres. In his will, Lord Crewe directed his trustees, Greville Howard of Levens Hall and William Fulke Greville of Battersea, to divert the entire rents and profits from the Cheshire and Staffordshire estates to his daughter, Elizabeth. He also favoured his numerous other relatives with bequests large and small, and even left £100 a year to each of his granddaughters. But his son, the second Baron Crewe, was to receive nothing [35].

When her grandfather died, young Annabel Crewe went to live at Madeley with her father's sister Elizabeth. Already in self-imposed exile at the chateau of Bois l'Evêque, near Liège in Belgium, the new Lord Crewe was not on speaking terms with Elizabeth and resented her taking responsibility for his daughter's upbringing. He sent a message to Annabel that he never wanted to see her again. And he never did. His family understood that he even failed to respond to the hint of a hike in the peerage to Earl of Offley and Viscount Madeley if he would return to vote in the critical passage of the Reform Bill in April and May 1832 [12].

Annabel's sister Henrietta sided with her father. She joined him in his Belgian fastness, and became a Roman Catholic. After he died in 1835, she returned to England and a life of withdrawn piety at Tiverton and later at Prior Park in Bath. Very occasionally, she visited Annabel at her Hill Street home in Mayfair.

Old Lord Crewe's will had made his daughter Elizabeth a wealthy woman. The portion left to her represented more than half of the total estate, both in area and value [12]. The Cheshire estates of almosr 8,000 acres were good dairy farmland. There were nearly 2,000 acres at both Barthomley and Warmingham; 1,000 at Elton; and smaller parcels of land at Weston, Gresty and Tetton (near Middlewich), Hale and Blacon, Crowton, Crewe, Madeley, Muxon (Mucklestone), North Rode, Sandbach, Spurstow, and Tetton. Land rents were producing around £1.0s.0d. per acre per year. Elizabeth's nett annual income from rents in the 1820s was over £10,000, the equivalent of well over £1,000,000 today. Tenancies included large farms like Crewe Gates with 350 acres, for which John Cliffe paid £357.2s.6d. yearly; and the small cottager like John Parrott, with ten perches of land for £4.4s.0d. yearly. Many holdings were of only three or four acres, held by assorted tradespeople, such as gamekeeper Thomas Beech, with three acres rent-free; shoemaker William Beck with six acres at £18.0s.0d. yearly; James Twemlow at Crewe Mill with 21 acres at £25.15s.0d. yearly; and the Overseer of the Poor, customarily appointed by his Lordship from amongst men of good local standing, with one acre at £6.12s.0d. yearly [36].

But there was a catch in old Lord Crewe's generosity to his daughter. In 1809, she had married Foster Cunliffe, son and heir of Sir Foster Cunliffe, Bart. As a condition of her father's will, both she and her husband had to abandon their married name and take *...the surname of 'Offley' with their own and quarter the arms of Offley with their arms...* [35].

The Cunliffe-Offleys, as they became, lived a placid life. They built a new home in the Regency style, on the site of a former house on the slopes of Bryn Wood Hill above Middle Madeley. Madeley Manor became a family home, second only to Crewe Hall: it is now a nursing home. In a survey of 1899 the Manor was described as *...a good family mansion, containing a dining room, library, billiard room, a very fine drawing room and about twenty one bedrooms...* It overlooked a landscaped setting of woodland and lake and was approached by a tree-lined carriageway where the drives from both west and east lodge gateways converged. *Life at Madeley must have been simple and easy, plenty of standard reading, friendly intercourse with neighbours and a great deal of gardening and visiting cottagers. In London they lived at 16, Upper Brooke Street in a small but pleasantly designed house...*which remained the Crewe town house until the lease expired in 1870 [12].

Foster Cunliffe-Offley *…was never in Parliament, but was an accomplished man of some talent in painting and a buyer of works of art in a moderate way. Some of his larger landscapes, not of great merit, have come down to us. His wife was musical and one sees her singing mentioned in contemporary memoirs* [12]. She dealt effectively with estate matters, from the welfare of retired staff to the letting of the shooting rights (in 1830, the Rev John Oldershaw of Stoke, Nantwich paid £30 for 4 years' sporting rights over Crewe land at Spurstow) [37]; negotiating lease renewals; and buying and selling shares in the developing railway companies. Although Hungerford, Elizabeth's young nephew, was away at school and then university, permanent staff were retained at Crewe Hall – but withdrawn at 5.00am for the day on 26 March 1832, so that the building would not be liable for Window and House Duty. Elizabeth's correspondence with her solicitor and agent, Mr EH Martin, reflects this quiet, shrewd, well-ordered life. For instance, on 22 July 1845 she wrote to Martin from Upper Brook Street that *…There has been a thunderstorm in the neighbourhood of London but not a drop of rain has fallen here. They say there is not a turnip in the county! I remain etc…* [37].

With such sound husbandry, the fortunes of the Crewes began to revive in the years immediately before Victoria came to the throne.

Chapter 6

TOWN AND COUNTRY

The Third Baron Crewe

'What curious attitudes he goes into!' 'Not at all,' said the King, '... those are Anglo-Saxon attitudes. He only does them when he's happy.[56]*'*

Hungerford Crewe (1812-1894) was born to an unhappy inheritance that probably inhibited him throughout his long life. His mother, Henrietta Walker-Hungerford Crewe died when he was eight years old. With his older sister Henrietta, who was then eleven, and his younger sister Annabel, who was only six, he went to live with his grandfather, the first Baron Crewe. Because their father was already estranged from the family and living in Belgium, Lord Crewe had the children made Wards of Chancery to secure their legal position.

The children lived at Crewe Hall alongside other relatives and a permanent household staff, although Annabel spent long periods with her aunt Elizabeth at Madeley Manor and in Rome. They spent an apparently carefree and probably under-disciplined childhood in the charge of tutors and governesses. *Hungerford, evidently an eccentric boy, was allowed to run loose and spent far too much time with servants and in the stables. One of his escapades...was to take a gun up to the farm when he was quite a small boy and to shoot a number of chickens. Playfellows were not lacking, as the cousins at Combermere, the Wellington Cottons, afterwards Lord Combermere comprised Caroline (who became Lady Downshire) and Meliora who were exact contemporaries and the families were very intimate...Another more distant neighbour was Hugh Cholmondeley (afterwards Lord Delamere) who was a great hero, being four years older than my mother . . . and close by at Betley Hall were the Tollet family* [12].

Hungerford was seventeen when his grandfather died in 1829. *He had quieted down to a peaceful sort of oddity, so that neither at school nor college was he removed for breaches of discipline. But he must have found routine study utterly difficult from the curious limitations of his mind, which was unable to apprehend anything whatever of any subjects of common knowledge to most people, but stored by constant repetition a good deal of information on others which appealed directly to his sentiments or interests. I fancy he rarely saw his father, who can have regarded him with nothing but contempt* [12]. Already a somewhat eccentric schoolboy, the balance of his mind at Eton cannot have been improved by

A Man of Property An idealised Hungerford Crewe, with the Hall behind him.

witnessing his tutor commit suicide. He went on to Christ Church, Oxford, but clearly was not an academic high-flyer. When he was 23, Hungerford became the third Baron Crewe on the death of his father, though he did not formally inherit the Crewe estates until two years later.

Crewe Hall nestled inside its own park of 575 acres. The extent of the regular staff at the Hall and its immediate estate is reflected in the production figures for the Hall's brewhouse. It only brewed each autumn, and in 1836 its September/November total was 984 gallons of ale and 906 gallons of beer [23]. The Hall and its grounds were insulated from the outside world by an estate of almost 1,000 acres leased to small farmers and cottagers, each with his own entry in Lord Crewe's rent record [36]. Here, in the wider estate, Hungerford Crewe faced serious responsibilities for such a young man. The shape of the estate holdings varied over the years as opportunities arose to acquire adjoining parcels of useful land; or the occasional need to meet a pressing financial demand was met by disposing of other acreage. Gross income from Hungerford Crewe's major estates in 1846 derived from Barthomley (£4,915); Warmingham (£3,830); Sandbach (£1,902); Blacon (£1,511); Spurstow (£853); and Peckforton Hall Farm (£590). Other income from leasing sporting rights, minor cottage and tenement rents, and sales of oak bark (for tanning), timber and hay from the estate and home farm, augmented the gross annual figure to approximately £14,000.

With admirable sense, Hungerford delegated day-to-day management of the Hall and estates to a competent Nantwich solicitor and self-employed land agent, Edward Hall Martin. Martin had acted for Hungerford's aunt, Mrs Cunliffe-Offley, but it is not known exactly when he began to handle Crewe Hall affairs, though a surviving cashbook makes clear that he was acting for Hungerford Crewe from 1844 to 1847 [38]. As a young man, Martin had been articled to the Nantwich solicitors Tomlinson and Welsby, and eventually succeeded to their practice. Judging by the extant cashbook, he appears to have run a well-regulated and efficient practice, assisted by his clerk Henry Davidson, to whom he paid an annual salary of £40.0s.0d. Influential and well-respected, the *indefatigable* Mr Martin lived at Henhull Cottage at Acton. He died on 25 January 1866 and was buried in Acton churchyard, but is commemorated in an inscribed lancet window in the north aisle of Nantwich parish church. On Mrs Martin's subsequent death, the window was embellished by the addition of Abel, Enoch and Noah to the hitherto solitary Job.

The following annual fees listed in the cashbook indicate that Martin had other clients among the local gentry and (perhaps of necessity) also acted for various Crewe connections: *Hungerford, Third Lord Crewe of Crewe Hall (£400); Mrs*

Tomkinson of Dorfold Hall (£200); The Hon Mrs E. Cunliffe-Offley of Madeley Manor (£40); Henry Brooke Esq., of Ashbrook Hall, Church Minshull (£40); The Revd Edward Hinchliffe, Rector of Barthomley (£12). The low fees from Mrs Cunliffe-Offley and Mr Hinchliffe reflect the former's status as the aunt of Lord Crewe, and the latter's as Rector of Barthomley, a living in Lord Crewe's gift. No wonder that Hinchliffe referred in print to his patron's *...upright, clever and indefatigable agent...*[8].

Martin used the services of the Nantwich and South Cheshire Bank, and later those of Dixon and Wardell of Chester. His monthly cash drawings were usually between £850 and £1,000, in amounts generally of £50 or £100 at a time, and rarely exceeding £200. This was the order of cash that was needed to attend to the routine business of Hungerford Crewe and his other clients. Martin was required to pay all outgoings for the household and estate, including those to builders for the extensive repair and building programme on the Cheshire estates; and to collect rents.

Martin's most complex duties lay in dealing with tenants over questions of leases, new building and alterations, and land improvement. In regard to the latter, Hungerford Crewe provided 'shells' (drainage pipes) for his farm tenants, and arranged bulk purchase of bone manure. All of this was doubtless reflected later in enhanced rental values. An instance of this investment in improvements is shown on 14 December 1844, when £278.4s.0d. was spent on trenching and draining shells at Elton, Crewe Green and Townhouse farms.

For the engrossment of some lease agreements, Martin used the services of Mr A McLure, a Nantwich solicitor. McLure was also the agent for the Norwich Union Fire Office, which Martin used for some of his clients' property. Many farm tenancies were granted on the basis of one, two or three 'lives': they would continue until the death of the tenant, or his next or the subsequent successor on the property. At the time of the death of a 'life', the landlord required a payment known as a heriot. Though relatively small amounts, these were regularly demanded by Mr Martin on behalf of Hungerford Crewe. An example of heriot payments is in three entries totalling 17s.6d. for 18 March 1846, and others on 10 March 1847. In the case of a lease extension, a heavier payment could be demanded. On 30 September 1846, £150 was required of John Lowe, a tenant at Elton, for the privilege of extending his lease from one 'life' to two 'lives'.

Rents were collected twice a year, at Lady Day and Michaelmas. Mr Martin's practice was to organise the collections in a suitable local hostelry where tenants would be entertained with (liquid) refreshments to make rent payments a little less unpalatable. For example, on 20 March 1846, £10.3s.10d. was paid to John

Cornes of the Bears Paw, Warmingham for entertaining tenants who were paying their rents. The rents collected totalled £1,946.3s.6d.

Tithe rents, payable for Astbury, Barthomley, Muxton (Mucklestone) and Warmingham totalled £3,925 for 1846. Rents totalling £5,240 on Madeley properties were collected on behalf of Mrs Cunliffe-Offley. Game rents for Elton, Sandbach, Tetton and Warmingham produced £92.0s.0d. in 1846. Additional income came from the occasional sale of standing timber, such as £345 from Quaker Coppice at Crewe Hall in April 1845.

Estate housing and buildings were well constructed and well maintained, and many remain in good condition. Hungerford's sense of responsibility towards the future environment, and for the continuing profitability of the estate in his own time and beyond, is illustrated by the payment of £5.0s.0d. to George Whitgrove on 23 January 1845 for planting oaks in the hedgerows in Warmingham.

Martin's brief seems to have extended to the purchase of stock for the home farm. Examples of this are two payments of £100 for sheep and bullocks, the latter on 7 October 1846 for a purchase to be made at Chester Fair. He paid meticulous attention even to small payments such as 8s.2d to blacksmith James Brereton on 8 January 1846 for shoeing horses, and £1.13s.3d to George Goodhall of Willaston on 3 November 1847 for thatch for the cottages in Hospital Street in Nantwich.

Responsibilities towards staff and tenantry were taken seriously. Widows of vicars and their offspring, orphans and the needy poor, were all provided for on a low but socially acceptable level of charity. There were many calls upon his Lordship's generosity, and each request was treated on its own merits. In July 1845, Lord Crewe allowed Ralph Poole ...*£1.4s.0d. To make up for the loss of his cow and calf*.... Many payments give a flavour of the times, such as those on 25 February 1846 of £20.0s.0d. for the Barthomley Christmas club; £5.0s.0d. for the Barthomley Men's Benefit: £5.0s.0d. for the Barthomley Sunday school and £5.0s.0d. for the Barthomley Children's Club. An entry of 24 June 1846 shows a payment of £1.5s.0d. to John Thompson, teacher at the Blue Cap School in Nantwich (an enterprise that Hungerford Crewe supported), but in 1860 this school was amalgamated into the new building of the Nantwich Grammar School. The new school was funded by £500 from George Fortescue Wilbraham of Delamere and £200 from Hungerford Crewe, who, with Martin, were three of the nine trustees whose two annual meetings were held at midsummer and on Christmas Day [16]. With the hindsight of history, these payments might be contrasted with payment on 9 June 1846 of Hungerford Crewe's annual subscription of £25 to the Cheshire Hunt.

For 200 years after the English Civil War, there had been little to disturb the equilibrium of rural south Cheshire, and the local dominance of the lords of the manor of Crewe. Things were rather different on the Crewes' Madeley estate where, as the area's most important land-owning family, they had already profited from industrialisation. Of the family holding of 4,125 acres, half were described as 'meadow', and about one third was arable, but coal, ironstone and limestone generated mineral wealth. Even in the 17th century, the Offleys had leased their mine at Leycett, an adjacent village to Madeley. In 1717, the iron-smelting furnace leased from John Crewe was producing 400 tons each year. Much of the output was utilised by the nail makers of south Staffordshire and south Lancashire. By 1840, the tithe schedule showed that 72% per cent of Madeley parish belonged to the Crewe family through their representative on earth, Mrs Cunliffe-Offley of Madeley Manor. Larger scale extraction of minerals at Leycett took place as the century unfolded and the Crewe Iron and Coal Company developed. A typical 21-year lease agreement for the mine in 1866 provided for annual rental of £600 and additional royalty payments on tonnage, plus cheap supplies of coal for Crewe Hall. By 1899, the collieries covered 230 acres of ground, producing good quality coal; the two main pits were Fair Lady and Bang-up. In addition, the availability of coal and clay allowed for a substantial brick and tile industry at Madeley. Over the years, the coal and iron resources added to the wealth of the local community. The Crewes were responsible landlords who provided many houses, a church in the village, and three schools in the locality - all built to last, and some still doing so, with the Crewe arms displayed on outside walls.

At it happened, Hungerford Crewe came into his inheritance just before similar social change began to impact profoundly on Crewe Hall itself. It began with the development of a national railway network. Within an astonishingly brief period, Hall and estate were propelled into the 19th century.

In 1837, the Grand Junction Railway, linking Warrington with Birmingham, bisected Madeley parish. The Crewes and other interested parties benefited from compensatory payments and the additional benefits of a private mineral line to bring coal and iron from Leycett to the sidings at Madeley. The line brought the steam engine within earshot of Crewe Hall. Hungerford Crewe, on the point of investing a lot of money and effort in upgrading the Hall, deferred his developments. While recognising the advantages of faster communication, he was unenthusiastic about the prospect of a burgeoning new industry on his doorstep. As he refused to sell any of his own estate, the railway company acquired the land for its track from a neighbouring landowner called Edleston.

The railway system expanded very rapidly. In 1840 the Crewe-Chester-Birkenhead link was established. When Nantwich and then Newcastle-under-Lyme each turned down the opportunity to become a railway junction, Monks Coppenhall was chosen instead and rechristened Crewe. By 1842, the Liverpool line converged at the same station.

The Grand Junction Railway Company wanted to redevelop its small works at Edge Hill in Liverpool on a green-field site. After making initial surveys at Winsford, the Company decided to build its new factory alongside the Chester railway line at Crewe. Production began in March 1843 with Mr F Trevithick as Locomotive Superintendent. Originally, the Works had been intended for the repair of engines, and occupied a limited area with only 161 staff. However, the Company soon started to build new locomotive engines at the Crewe Works, starting in February 1845 with 'Columbine'. According to legend, Hungerford Crewe's standard direction to his coachman at the start of impromptu drives in his carriage was *Anywhere, but the New Works!*

The Grand Junction Railway had already absorbed the Liverpool and Manchester Railway. In 1846, it amalgamated with the London and Birmingham, and the Manchester and Birmingham, Railways to create the London and North Western Railway. Crewe became the headquarters of its Northern Division. By this time, the area of the Works had increased to 30 acres, and the number of staff to 600 (and to 1,100 by 1847, and 1,600 by 1848). The railway station was extended in 1848 on a site next to the Manchester line, behind the Crewe Arms Hotel. Hungerford Crewe sold the land to the LNW Railway Company for £3,000, on condition that a private siding would be provided for Crewe Hall coal supplies [39].

By 1851, the population of the town of Crewe was 5,000 and rising. To cope with this growth, the Railway Company needed to build houses for its workers. The first 32 cottages in the centre of the old town had been built and occupied by the end of 1842. By 1848 there were 520, and by 1858 well over 700.

The North Staffordshire Railway Company persuaded Hungerford to sell some land for the new line planned between Crewe and the Potteries. The deal included compensation of £1,000 for inconvenience paid in November 1847; and the construction and maintenance of cattle crossings [39]. But the opening of the new line in October 1848 brought the railway uncomfortably close to Crewe Hall, and Hungerford was unhappy with its intrusion on his privacy. He was also irritated by the increasing number of inquisitive townsfolk passing close to Crewe Hall along the old road (later the Stowford drive) from Crewe Gates through Stowford to Weston. In part, these problems were overcome by the construction of the new Weston Lane (now Weston Road) in 1849. There had been a turnpike road from

Nantwich to the Grand Trunk Canal at Wheelock since 1816, but the Potteries now needed direct access to the railway junction at Crewe. The Turnpike Trustees and the Grand Junction Railway obtained a Turnpike Act in 1848, and borrowed £2,000 from Hungerford on the strength of it. The straight new road ran direct from Crewe station to Weston and Newcastle-under-Lyme on a tree-screened route half a mile distant from Crewe Hall [39]. It admirably served the needs of all parties but Nantwich, whose local importance waned accordingly.

In January 1861, the North Staffordshire Railway Company paid Hungerford £805.7s.6d (or 2s.6d, per square yard) for a further one and one third acres of land for sidings [40]. Still Lord Crewe fretted for his privacy, and in 1864 he planted further trees along a belt one and a quarter miles long, to mask the North Staffs Railway embankment *now so conspicuous from the new approach to the Hall* [41].

Hungerford Crewe was a very wealthy and respected landowner, and was for a period a Deputy Lieutenant of Cheshire. A national survey of landowners in 1873 showed that the county of Cheshire was the fourth county in England with the greatest proportion of land area tied up in landed estates [14]. Just forty people owned something over half of the whole of Cheshire. Of these, the Duke of Westminster at Eaton Hall, the Earl of Stamford at Dunham Massey, Lord Stanley at Alderley Park, the Marquess of Cholmondeley at Cholmondeley Castle, Lord Egerton at Tatton Park, Lord Tollemache at Peckforton Castle and seven other peers owned 26% of the area of the county. Thirteen peers had a seat in Cheshire and a London house [23].

Hungerford's immediate family seem to have regarded him with tolerant affection. His tenants accepted this awkward, shy, religious neurotic and gruff, autocratic landlord as being reasonable as any other landlord of his time, and regarded his eccentricities with modest pride. They appreciated the balance of stability and progressive development that he brought to the estate. His peculiarities certainly made good stories. His great-niece Lady Cynthia Colville recounts how a *shooting party guest...broke a large Sèvres vase at Crewe Hall but was not immediately admonished. However, at breakfast next morning he was told by Hungerford, 'There is no hurry, the carriage won't be round for half an hour and that will give you plenty of time to catch your train!'* When an elderly visitor slipped and fell down a complete flight of stairs at Crewe Hall, her sycophantic husband rushed up to his host saying *Lord Crewe, I do hope my wife hasn't injured your beautiful staircase* [34]! Hungerford had little sense of time. A very late bed-goer, he would sit for hours, half asleep, in the Oak Parlour while his faithful valet Hickman waited to help him undress and go to bed. One bright summer morning at 6.00am, just as the gardeners were starting to mow the lawns, he rang for Hickman and said *'Nobody need sit up for me!'*

There is no evidence that Hungerford ever spoke in the House of Lords, or that he compared with his sister's cultured, articulate husband, Richard Monckton-Milnes. However, he was invested as a Fellow of the Society of Antiquaries in 1840, and a Fellow of the Royal Society the following year; and Gladstone - no intellectual slouch - invited himself to Crewe Hall on at least one occasion. Moreover, those around Hungerford helped to make up for any intellectual deficiencies. One of these was John Ellerton, whom Hungerford appointed to the living of St Michael's Church, Crewe Green in 1860, and who remained the incumbent until 1872. Adopting Scholefield's tune 'St Clement', Ellerton wrote the well-known hymn 'The day thou gavest, Lord, is ended'.

Above all, Hungerford understood his own best interests in matters great and small. Writing to his sister Annabel in 1857, he explained that *I cannot very well lend you my carriage on Saturday – at present my Stable is by no means complete - President (one of my horses) Harvey Greville has declined as a gift. When I leave Town I have sold him for £17 to a horse dealer. I have only two horses in Town - suitable for Harness (President one of them) I could lend you the Barouche for half an hour Tomorrow - I have bought another Carriage Horse he ought not to be Hard worked for nearly another year. Your husband has spoken to me about the Carriage, last evening at the House and again this evening in Upper Brook Street. You see how I am situated I have not a Stable full of Horses eating the Bread of Idleness. I dine out on Saturday and want the Brougham myself under these circumstances. Excuse me* [42].

In compliance with a requirement of his grandfather's will, Hungerford had to offer the first refusal of vacant church livings in his gift to *lineal descendants of his brothers or sisters.* Deeply religious, Hungerford had sometimes to make such offers to relatives who were not to his liking as parsons or as men. He became influenced by the High Church tendency of the Oxford Movement. In 1852-54, he had replaced the 13th century chancel and many of the older internal fittings at Barthomley parish church. The advowson of Barthomley was traditionally in the ownership of the Lord of the Manor. Not surprisingly, several Rectors of Barthomley had been, and were to be, relatives of the Crewes, including William de Praers (1315), Robert Fouleshurst (1475), Walter Offley (1704), Joseph Crewe DD (1739), Randulph Crewe LLD (1758), Offley Crewe MA (1777), Charles Crewe MA (1782), and Willoughby Crewe LLB (1819). Indeed, the family had purchased some livings - which at various times included Madeley, Mucklestone, Nantwich and Warmingham, as well as Barthomley – as a means of support for poor relations. But they purchased others as investments. For example, on 2 February 1734 John Crewe-Offley paid John Amson the modest sum of £4,500 for the deeds of title to the church and advowson of

'Lay Episcopacy' A caricatured Hungerford Crewe by 'Spy' (Leslie Ward) in 'Vanity Fair' in January 1882.

Astbury near Congleton [43]. By 1816, the annual income of Astbury church was £6,000: a lucrative return on their investment at a time of low inflation.

However, finding Barthomley too remote for his regular Sunday attendance, or that of his growing tenantry, Hungerford decided to build a church nearer Crewe Hall. Sir George Gilbert Scott (1811-78), best-known as the architect of the Foreign and Commonwealth Office, the Albert Memorial and the Midland Grand Hotel, St Pancras, chanced to be restoring Nantwich parish church. Hungerford therefore commissioned as design from him for St. Michael's church at Crewe Green, north west of the Hall and about a mile from Crewe town. A Sandbach builder, John Stringer, erected the church in 1857-58; and Thomas Bower, a Nantwich architect, later designed the adjacent church school of 1882.

Hungerford trusted some of his key staff to attend to minor payments on his behalf and Mr Martin was authorised to provide them with cash 'floats', which were reconciled at the end of each month. In 1846, central personnel at Crewe Hall and their annual salaries (where known) were Arthur Campbell, Bailiff (£80); George Slynn, Head Gamekeeper (£40); James Mackenzie, Head Gardener; Edward Harper, House Carpenter; Mr Duga, Butler; and Mrs Duga, Housekeeper. Each of these was responsible for paying staff in the individual departments. For instance, Mrs Duga received £91.17s.8d. on 12 January 1846 for the monthly

Station in Life Lord Crewe's private sidings at Crewe Station in 1881. The clearly rural lane behind the platform leads to Crewe Hall.

household requirements, and a further £50.10s.5d. for wages for herself and the other female staff for the period from Michaelmas to Christmas 1845. Similarly, on the same date, Mr Duga received £35.9s.6d. for his household expenditure, and £36.15.0. for wages for himself and the male staff for the period from Michaelmas to Christmas 1845. Lower servants received low wages. George Stringer, under keeper, was paid 12s.0d. per week in January 1845, and the Crewe Hall postman, Robert Harding, was paid £2.10s.0d. for a quarter's wages on 30 September 1846, although he did receive a pair of 'top boots' £2.2s.0d. on the same date. Harding had previously received a new hat on 20 September 1844, purchased for £1.1s.0d, from Mrs M Carrington of Nantwich. A reasonable estimate of the annual outgoing in respect of the Crewe Hall establishment of the 1840s, together with its Park and Home Farm, would be of the order of £2,000.

When Hungerford was in London, Crewe Hall was left in the care of his servants, and the 1861 census return recorded ten permanent residents at Crewe Hall: John Miller, Butler (47); Wm. Duckworth, Footman (18); J. Barleycorn, Steward's Room Boy (16); Edward Povey, Groom (18); Mabel Mason, Housekeeper (63); Mary Atwell, Still Room Maid (36); Mary Harrison, Dairy Maid (26); Mary Mellor, Laundrymaid (34); Caroline A. Barnett, under House-maid (26); and Caroline Woodford, House-maid (32).

By the time of the next Census in 1871, the number of household staff had risen to fourteen. The addition of two lady's maids, an under butler and a valet suggests an upgrading of the household staff and their duties. There is no record of Mr Knee, the butler, who was possibly with his master in London at the time. Other key workers who did not live in the Hall but were employed at the time, included Benjamin Dunkley, house carpenter; John Bloor, farm carpenter; Charles Austin, gas fitter; George Slynn, gamekeeper; William Hartley, coachman; and other lesser servants who lived in the many estate cottages. William Whittaker, head gardener, and his wife Margaret lived in the Gardens Cottage with Bridget Cody their domestic servant. There were also five gardeners living at the stables.

When Hungerford inherited the property, he had embarked on a career of estate building, much of which remains. Some of the large sums of money transferred by Mr Martin to Lord Crewe's account with the London bankers, Smith, Payne and Smith, were probably to clear outstanding accounts with the builders employed during this reconstruction. At the Hall, Nantwich architect George Latham had carried out minor renovations to chimneys and alterations to the library in 1836 [44]. Latham also suggested the warm-air heating system that was introduced in 1837 [44]. Evidence of this exists in several fretted brass grilles in skirting around the building, and in the cavities of the complex and low-roofed north cellars which house remnants of a coal chute and boiler room. In a further room was pipe ducting, operating a heat exchange system similar to a Roman hypocaust - and, by modern standards, just about as effective.

However, these alterations were only the prelude to a much larger scheme for which Hungerford commissioned the services of Edward Blore (1787-1879). Blore's reputation as a reliable but economical architect had led the Government to employ him in 1832 to complete Buckingham Palace after Nash was dismissed for extravagance [45]. Blore had also carried out work at Windsor Castle and Hampton Court. Between 1827 and 1849, he was Surveyor to Westminster Abbey, where he refitted the choir. His work in Cheshire had included improvements to Capesthorne Hall and Vale Royal Abbey; and he went on to design Great Moreton Hall for Mr GH Ackers.

Between 1837 and 1842, Blore undertook a large-scale internal restoration of Crewe Hall and its stables. This cost around £30,000 - equivalent to well over £2,000,000 at today's values, even though the Hall could still boast only one bathroom when all the work was finished. The project included the conversion of the open central courtyard to a single storey marble hall and the insertion of an approach to the main staircase from the west side. The RIBA collections include 232 working drawings by Blore for repairs to Crewe Hall, and Cambridge University Library houses Edward Blore's Account Books for 1840-50, with many references to Crewe, and two volumes of his Crewe Hall wages books. The earlier, coarser Jacobean decoration was elaborated to early Victorian standards. Ceilings and plasterwork in the library and drawing room were embellished, and some chimneypieces were added. Surviving the 1866 fire, the dining room has a chimneypiece by Blore with original 17th century overmantel carving of the Relief of Plenty.

A tower with turret clock was added to the stables block on the east side of the quadrangle, with a mechanism dated 1851. Blore also designed the Sandbach (later Slaughter Hill) lodge on the north side of Crewe Hall Park in 1847. The estate farms and cottages were improved, using local labour and materials. One such job in October 1844 required 41,674 bricks made locally at Church Minshull by Charles Egerton at a cost of £9.14s.7d [38].

Hungerford Crewe also employed William Andrews Nesfield (1793-1881) to carry out a substantial landscaping restoration scheme around Crewe Hall in the 1840s and 1850s [46]. Nesfield's first report in February 1842 proposed to partly restore some of the boundary walls of the formal gardens immediately surrounding the house, and introduce parterres and gravel walks with stone steps and statuary. *An iron fence attached by stout stone posts will enclose the present lawn. Grass plot on the centre of court edged with a stone kerb and surmounted by a column bearing a globe Dial. High standard roses trained on umbrella wires. Yucca gloriosa. Irish Yew. Standard Portugal laurels (kept low). Compartments of Beds (for the lowest species of herbaceous plants) edged with Box upon gravel. Circular plots having large urns on high pedestals. Arbor Vitae forming squares on the circles. Low vases on pedestals placed on circles or scrolls of grass. Red cedars. Grass scallops having statues on high pedestals. Lions on oblong pedestals...as the North front of the house is overshadowed, this portion of the Parterre will not be congenial to herbaceous plants, therefore various devices are here adopted in grass and Box upon gravel and with the addition of architectural objects as Statues, Vases etc., much rich and appropriate variety will be gained. Symmetrical and other figures will be formed with outlines of low Box. The old Masters filled the intervals with different coloured sand, but small light coloured pebbles will do better set in Mulgrave cement.*

Remnants of much of Nesfield's work can still be traced, and is clear from photographs of the grounds taken after the 1870 restoration. The Nesfield design for the north parterre at Crewe was published in the Royal Horticultural Society's 'Gardeners Chronicle' of 7 December 1863. The ornate parterres required vast maintenance, suggesting that Crewe Hall had one of the finest Victorian gardens in the county between the 1840s and the 1920s [46].

Nesfield undertook his duties thoroughly, even selecting a head gardener in September 1855 because he considered the appointment essential to the planting and maintenance of his elaborate scheme. A Mr Veitch and Sir William Hooker, Nesfield's friend, gave testimonials for a William Whittaker, whose appointment Nesfield recommended. Despite misgivings that Whittaker was a Roman Catholic - considered sinister in the light of the controversial restoration of the Catholic hierarchy in 1850, and guilty-by-association with Irish fenianism - Hungerford Crewe appointed him. By April, 1856, Whittaker was making his mark at Crewe, as Nesfield wrote to Hungerford: *...pleased to see improvement in the Kitchen Garden . . . had also had time to look through the shrubbery where Whittaker is removing superfluous plants which Mackenzie roguishly introduced....*

Hungerford evidently enjoyed his pleasure grounds and the walled garden at Crewe Hall where his particular interest was the rare orchids that Whittaker grew for him. He always wore one in his buttonhole, even when dressed in the scarlet uniform of a Deputy Lieutenant.

From 1856 to 1866, Hungerford generally used the architectural services of Nesfield's son, (William) Eden Nesfield. Eden Nesfield ensured the consistent style of estate house building that has survived to the present day. His work for Lord Crewe began with a memorial monument in 1856 for the family grave at

Grand Designs (I) WA Nesfield's plan for the parterre in front of the north elevation of Crewe Hall...

Grand Designs (II) ...and the reality, photographed in 1870

Barthomley Church. More interesting examples of his work are the later lodges and cottages on the estate. Of these, the most notable are the Weston (now golden gates) lodge, and the Barthomley lodge.

Between the golden gates lodge and Crewe railway station, Eden Nesfield also built Fir Tree Cottage (1865) and the farmhouse at the brow of the rise in the road. His most attractive contributions to estate housing are the stylised semi-detached Stowford Cottages (1864-5) immediately east of the golden gates lodge. When he designed them, Eden Nesfield was in partnership with Richard Norman Shaw.

But disaster struck. In the early hours of Wednesday 3 January 1866, the Hall was ravaged by a serious fire. The following day, 'The Times' reported that *Crewe Hall, Cheshire, the seat of Lord Crewe, was destroyed by fire yesterday morning. The greater portion of this splendid mansion, including the reception rooms, is completely gutted. The servants' offices, stabling, and outhouses, with the furniture, pictures, and plate, are saved. The fire is supposed to have originated in the carelessness of one of the servants.* In fact, although subsequent reports conflict with each other, the conflagration was thought to have started when a wooden beam caught fire in one of the three fireplaces that were then located in the long gallery. Except for the dining room, the main reception rooms were gutted, but the walls of the Hall remained intact. Fortunately, there was no loss of life, and there was time to save many of the important paintings and *objets d'art*. The story goes that, while the Hall was still in flames, Hungerford telegraphed Edward Blore (not, as his niece later recorded, Edward Barry) and William Twopenny …*Crewe is now burning; come and build it up again!*

Locally and nationally, friends and well-wishers expressed their sympathy. The Bishop of Lichfield, the Marquess of Lansdowne, Sir Ralph Sneyd of Keele Hall, Lady Ellesmere, Lord Curzon and others sent letters.. The Marquess (and future Duke) of Westminster asked Hungerford to *let me write one line of very sincere and hearty condolence on the most calamitous destruction of the grand old house, which we must all feel, while we sympathise with you, what a loss to the country, for nothing can replace the beautiful workmanship of olden time - with your care of it and thorough appreciation of its beauty, besides having so admirably restored it you must be almost overwhelmed with grief.* Catherine Gladstone (wife of the incumbent chancellor of the exchequer and future premier) added a practical note: *Pray remember that Hawarden Castle is open and ready to receive you if it can help. I hope you and the Houghtons have not been made ill.*

Hungerford inserted a notice in the 'Chester Record' shortly afterwards, stating that *Lord Crewe is desirous of publicly testifying his obligation to the zeal and activity of his establishment and his neighbours during the conflagration of Crewe Hall on Wednesday Morning, the 3rd of January by which many family memorials and valuable articles of property were preserved.*

After the fire, Crewe Hall was largely uninhabitable. In a characteristically eccentric move, Lord Crewe took up temporary residence with Mr and Mrs Whittaker at the Gardens Cottage. His sister Annabel agreed in a letter that this would be much more congenial to him than the Crewe Arms (*...that noisy hotel...*). He would be able to enjoy his walled garden and the conservatories, and Mrs Whittaker seemed pleased to squeeze him into her little parlour.

In the dozen years that followed, Hungerford and his architect Edward Barry went on to transform Crewe Hall into a country home of some importance. Their relationship and the house they created are a separate story. As his great-niece wrote many years later *...Crewe grew up to a lonely old age and his interests and affections were centred on his house and property which became to him as a wife and child* [34].

Paradoxically, Crewe Hall only came into its own after Hungerford Crewe had died, when it became an opulent backcloth to his nephew's glittering political career.

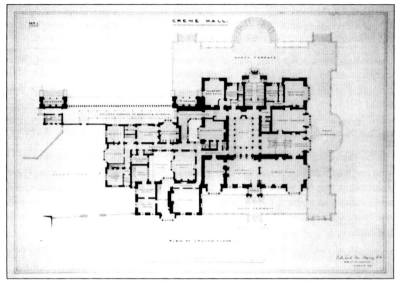

Grand Designs (III) Edward Barry's 1871 design for rebuilding the ground floor of Crewe Hall.

Grand Designs (IV) Edward Barry's 1871 drawing for rebuilding the south elevation of Crewe Hall.

Chapter 7

FIRST AND LAST

The Marquess of Crewe

It was the upper classes, not the lower, that cracked[57].

A terminal bout of influenza carried off the octogenarian Hungerford Crewe at New Year, 1894. His heir was his sister's son, the second Baron Houghton - Robert Offley Ashburton Milnes (1858-1945).

In 1861, Hungerford's sister Annabel had married Richard Monckton Milnes. Monckton Milnes was an author, poet, politician, international traveller, first biographer of Keats, and all-round man of letters. He was also a bibliomaniac, who amassed a library of 24,000 volumes which reputedly included Europe's largest collection of pornography[47]. Presumably he kept the latter well out of sight of his staider house guests, such as the Archbishop of York; in any event, his son quickly sold this part of his inheritance, which is now in the British Library.

Richard Monckton Milnes The first Baron Houghton, Lord Crewe's father

Created Baron Houghton in 1863, Monckton Milnes had the expensive tastes of a wealthy man without the wealth to pay for them. The Houghton family seat, Fryston Hall near Pontefract in Yorkshire, suffered a fire in 1876 and its restoration strained his finances. Having humorously predicted *...that my exit will be the result of too many entrées...*he died of a heart attack after eating and drinking not wisely but too well at Vichy in 1885.

The Houghtons had two daughters, Amicia and Florence, and a son, Robert. Florence was born during the Crimean War, and named after Monckton Milnes' friend, Florence Nightingale, whom he had persistently sought to marry in his youth.

Robert was born at the Houghtons' London house, 16 Upper Brook Street, when his parents were already into their middle years. He spent his early life in Mayfair and at Fryston, but regularly visited his uncle Hungerford at Crewe Hall with his mother and sisters. He later described how he, his sisters and their young friends enjoyed boisterous games in the long gallery on winter afternoons, well away from the scary presence of 'Uncle Crewe' in the oak parlour [12]. As a boy of eight, he was present when Crewe Hall caught fire in January 1866.

Robert excelled at poetry at Harrow, and progressed to Trinity College, Cambridge, graduating in 1879. He also travelled extensively with his father in the United States and Europe. In 1880, when he was 22, he married Sibyl Marcia Graham. A member of Brooks and Boodle's clubs, Robert moved in London Society, but remained modest, well-liked and personable, with an enthusiasm for politics. Despite Lord Houghton's representations on his son's behalf to Gladstone, who was conveniently placed as both family friend and Prime Minister, Robert had to wait three years until the right opportunity presented itself. In April 1883, he became one of the four personal secretaries to the Foreign Secretary, Lord Granville. Contemporary events in Egypt and the Sudan, including the fall of Khartoum and the death of General Gordon, served as a useful apprenticeship for Robert in politics, diplomacy and colonial affairs.

In the era before hereditary peerages could be renounced, his father's death in 1885 thwarted Robert's hopes of becoming a Liberal MP. Now Lord Houghton, he became a Liberal Whip in the Upper House. The defeat of Gladstone's Liberals over Irish Home Rule in October 1886 put the Conservatives in power. Out of office, the Houghtons planned a visit to India where their friends, Lord and Lady Dufferin, were Viceroy and Vicereine. The trip was not taken, and in September 1887, while her children were convalescing from scarlet fever at Crewe Hall with Uncle Crewe, Sybil Houghton caught the disease herself and died at the age of 30.

Bereaved and desolate, Robert spent time re-assessing his life. He knew that when Hungerford Crewe died he would inherit the comfortable fortunes of Crewe Hall and its estates. As the Liberals had no immediate prospects of returning to Government, he decided to study estate management at the Royal Agricultural College. In 1888, Cirencester did not have the bucolic *chic* that it has since acquired; and in any case Robert fell ill and quit the course on medical advice. For the sake of his health, he travelled to Egypt and Italy, seeking solace in literature and the composition of some morbid poetry. He was abroad during the winter of 1889-1890 when he learned in South Africa that his only son, Richard, had died at the age of eight.

Back home, he worked in the House of Lords as one of the few energetic peers available to the Liberals now that many territorial magnates had defected to the Liberal Unionists over Irish Home Rule. Gladstone returned to office in August 1892 and, through Queen Victoria, Robert was asked to become Viceroy (Lord Lieutenant) of Ireland. As the formal and public representative of the Queen, he would be responsible in Dublin for upholding the pomp and ceremony of her court. His biographer, James Pope-Hennessy, described the job as a 'shop window' position because it was ultimately accountable on all significant political issues to whichever MP chanced to be incumbent Chief Secretary for Ireland in the cabinet. It was also a physical risk because politicians and staff at Dublin Castle remained occasional targets of nationalist attacks.

Nonetheless, Robert would be responsible for keeping the Queen and her Government regularly informed of Irish opinion, and the effective handling of all matters Irish was crucial to Gladstone's political - and perhaps his emotional - survival. As Robert was a committed 'Home Ruler', from most points of view it was a great honour for a man still only 34 years old.

The post did not come cheap. Robert had carriages and horses shipped to Dublin, and state liveries designed for his household staff. He was accompanied by twelve equerries, and his grooms of the chamber walked backwards from him. A retiring man, he wore the £20,000 Irish diamond insignia with diffidence. His public duties included hosting levées for 600 guests, as well as regular balls and other functions. Fortunately, his sister Florence (by now Mrs Henniker, and wife of a none-too-wealthy army officer) would sometimes act as his hostess at Dublin Castle, which was where she began an intense friendship with the novelist Thomas Hardy.

After a cabinet dispute over naval estimates in 1894, Gladstone resigned the premiership. (The Grand Old Man died four years later. Before her own death in 1985, in her 101st year, Crewe's daughter Celia was the last surviving person to have known him.) Lord Rosebery succeeded Gladstone as Prime Minister, but the Conservatives won the general election the following year. Meanwhile, Morley had persuaded Roseberry to recommend to Queen Victoria that she should elevate Robert from a barony to an earldom. This recognised his public work in Ireland over the previous three years. Moreover, it coincided with the death of Uncle Crewe, who had bequeathed him the vast Crewe inheritance. Robert's chosen title - Earl of Crewe - was inevitable. So was his change of family surname to Crewe-Milnes.

Out of office, the new Lord Crewe remained politically active, working to hold his squally party together. He also moved in a social set that included Albert Edward, Prince of Wales (later King Edward VII). They shared an enthusiasm for shooting and racing. Fryston Hall was used for Leger Week and other Doncaster race meetings, although Robert lived chiefly at Crewe Hall at this time. His second marriage, in Westminster Abbey on 15 April 1899, created a sensation in London Society. He was 41, and his bride, Margaret ('Peggy') Primrose, was 18 - only eight months older than his eldest daughter, Annabel. Peggy's father was

Child Bride Lady Margaret ('Peggy') Primrose photographed for the 'Illustrated London News' in April 1899 at the time of her marriage to Lord Crewe.

Lord Roseberry, and her mother had become the richest woman in Britain when her own father, Baron Mayer de Rothschild, died. Rosebery regarded Robert as a competent politician but a halting speaker: apocryphally, when he heard that his pregnant daughter was in labour, Rosebery expressed the hope that her delivery would be quicker than her husband's. The Crewes made their London home at Uncle Crewe's old town house at 23, Hill Street, Berkeley Square, but in 1901 they bought Wharncliffe House in Curzon Street, renaming it Crewe House. It became celebrated for their lavish entertaining; Winston Churchill met his future wife there. Robert sold Fryston Hall shortly afterwards, and it was later demolished.

At this period, Crewe Hall was under-used and on 29 March 1902 'Country Life' advertised it to let: *...It contains eight reception rooms, four other sitting rooms, 26 principal bedrooms and dressing rooms, four bathrooms and offices which have lately been remodelled on the most modern system and is provided with the newest sanitation with electric light and gas and a private PO telephone. There is good stabling for 27 horses and the best meets of the Cheshire and North Stafford hounds are within easy reach. The gardens and glasshouses are extensive and the grounds, which are of great beauty, are ornamented by a lake of 61 acres. Land, pasture or tillage may be let with the house at the option of the tenant. The shooting of the coverts and over an Estate of about 4,150 acres, to which other shootings might be added to this area, would be included...*

Lord Crewe photographed at the time of his second marriage.

When the Liberals returned to power in 1905, the new Prime Minister, Sir Henry Campbell-Bannerman, selected Robert as Lord President of the Council, and later recommended him for the Garter. HH Asquith, who succeeded the dying Campbell-Bannerman in 1908, appointed Crewe as Leader of the House of Lords and Secretary of State for the Colonies. Six months later, he became in addition Lord Privy Seal, and in 1909 accompanied King Edward VII's royal party to Berlin as Minister-in-Attendance. Crewe retained the Privy Seal when he became Secretary of State for India, temporarily in 1910 and permanently the following year. At the India Office, he was party to the announcement by the new King-Emperor, George V, at his coronation durbar, that the subcontinent's capital was to be transferred to a new city at Delhi. On the King's personal initiative, the Crewe peerage had been raised from Earldom to Marquesate in the coronation honours list (a promotion that the *Earl* of Crewe public house in Nantwich road ignored until the day it closed, a century later). In the same year, the Crewes' son, Jack, was born. Crewe House was almost destroyed by fire.

In April 1913, the King and Queen Mary accepted Crewe's invitation to stay at the Hall for three nights during a royal visit to south Cheshire and the Potteries. This remains the most distinguished occasion in the Hall's history, and required extensive (and expensive) preparation. The royal party arrived by train to a military band and a reception by county and local dignitaries. A series of industrial visits filled their days: to the London and North Western Railway Company's

Old Retainer Benjamin Dunkley (born 1832) was house carpenter at the Hall from 1869 until his death in 1917.

Crewe Works; to the Colclough, Copeland, Doulton, Fielding, Meakin, Minton, Ridgeway, and Wedgwood Potteries; and to two or three mills and a colliery. Local dignitaries were greeted at each stopping place. The meticulous programme notes provided *...for the morning of Wednesday, 23 April 1913, 10.15 a.m. Leave Crewe in Motors, slowing down through Audley (stopping while schoolchildren sing one verse of the National Anthem) and Chesterton, and via Newcastle (not stopping)...'*

Each evening, the King and Queen returned to Crewe Hall and the superlative food for which the Crewes were noted, and the glees sung - possibly less than superlatively - by local choirs. King and Consort were not accommodated in the (damask) state bedroom with its exposed windows on the south front of the Hall. They slept in the chintz bedroom which faced west under the tower, with windows less vulnerable to any suffragettes with stones to throw.

The King and Queen planted ceremonial trees, supervised respectively by Mr Whittaker, the Head Outside Gardener, and Mr Spence, the Head Inside Gardener. The King's Spanish chestnut flourished, but decades later fell in the cause of progress and an industrial packing hall. The Queen's tree died of natural causes soon after it was planted.

On the final evening of the visit, the band of Foden's Motor Works gave a concert for the royal party. Afterwards, the King told the conductor of the pleasure that the concert had given him, and commanded the band to play again the following morning before the return to London. And so they did, serenading the royal porridge from the north terrace below the bay window in the long gallery [46].

Royal Visit (I) TM King George V and Queen Mary stay at Crewe Hall in April 1913. Back row, left to right: Hon Neil Primrose MP (Lady Crewe's brother); Lady Sybil Primrose (Lady Crewe's sister); unidentified; unidentified; Lord Derby; HM The King; Lord Crewe; Hon Arthur O'Neill MP (Lord Crewe's son-in-law); Clive Coates (Lord Crewe's son-in-law); unidentified. Front row, left to right: Lady Cleveland (Lady Crewe's grandmother); unidentified; Lady Crewe; Lord Madeley (Lord and Lady Crewe's son); HM The Queen; Lady Annabel O'Neill (Lord Crewe's eldest daughter); Lady Cynthia Colville (Lord Crewe's younger twin daughter); Lady Celia Coates (Lord Crewe's elder twin daughter); Mrs Arthur Henniker (Lord Crewe's sister).

When Lord Crewe inherited Crewe Hall in 1894, it had eighteen family and guest bedrooms, many with adjoining dressing rooms. Each had a distinctive name. 'Damask' was the principal guest bedroom. The south-facing 'Cain and Abel' bedroom was so called because of the grotesque stone representation on the chimneypiece. The 'Rosebud' bedroom had lost its attractive westerly outlook, and was converted into a lobby where an enormous, double-doored Chubb wall-safe was located. The other bedrooms were called blue, boat, buff, chapel, chintz, fruit, mulberry, Nantwich, north, parsons, pink, red, south, white, and yellow. Nonetheless, Lord Crewe hankered after even more bedrooms. He also sought advice from George Plucknett, Cubitt's London manager, on relocating the kitchens to eliminate cooking smells. Both problems had a common solution. In 1896, the Nantwich architect, Thomas Bower, designed a modest extension to the west wing, providing additional space on both floors to the west end of the south elevation for bedrooms, nurseries, and schoolroom. At the same time, new kitchens and services were provided in the basement.

The east-facing room in the ground floor of the 18th century south-west wing was converted from kitchen to book room, and later to billiards room, with adjacent lavatories and washroom. To provide a bird's eye view of the game, the billiards room had a narrow first-floor balcony round two sides, approached by a small winding staircase.

The extended house needed more servants. The housekeeper's inventory for the period 1876 to 1890 listed 32 servants' bedrooms: for butler, housekeeper, two ladies' maids, cook, valet, footman, steward's boy, two laundry maids, upper house maid, four house maids, two kitchen maids, still room maid, dairy maid, seven men servants, groom, coachman, foreman, upper gardener, under gardener and helper. Other male servants and gardeners were accommodated in the stables.

In large houses like Crewe Hall, the servants went about their duties virtually unheard and unseen. It was completely out of the question for them to use the main staircase unless their duties took them there, so there were separate stairs for their use. Before the 1870 reconstruction, there had been a single servants' staircase in the north west corner of the old house. After the reconstruction, which provided additional servants' bedrooms in the attics, one spiral staircase was installed for the designated use of the men servants and another for female servants. The two routes were distinct and separate and a brick wall at the top separated the two suites of bedrooms.

The housekeeper's inventory reveals the household organisation of the Hall, and its standard of furnishing [47]. Meticulously kept in copper plate manuscript entries, it lists the contents of each room, large and small, valuable and mundane. From brushing room to cook's bedroom, from clock room to dairy, from damask dressing room to fire guard closet, from fruit bedroom to gardener's room, from gallery lobby to housekeeper's room, from raw-meat larder to still room - every single portable item was recorded.

The eight Reynolds oil paintings that graced the walls of the drawing room are itemised, as are the family portraits in the long gallery; but so are the *iron bedsteads with striped linen hangings* in the second maid's bedroom. The valuable contents of the china room are separate from the extensive schedule of display china, and list the Dresden, Minton and Sèvres dinner services alongside the Masons Ironstone. Down in the servants' hall is the *22 feet long one-piece Oak Table* with four wooden forms plus an *Ale Wagon and twelve Horns*. The linen list covers table damask, bedsheets, towels, napkins and items for household use. Most linen items are laundry marked and referenced, and the best table linen has purchase dates going back over thirty years. Good husbandry begat good housekeeping.

The schedules of silver and silver plate are formidable. From 25 inch oval venison dishes, the silver plated serving dishes progress through 65 more of varying dimensions before reaching 93 dinner forks, old pattern; 96 dinner forks, new pattern; 160 tablespoons; 70 dessert spoons; 67 dessert forks; and so on. In the butler's pantry, there was a purpose built strong room (removed in the late 1970s) where silver and plate for his lordship's table were kept secure before issue to the service area through a hatch at the east end of the ground floor corridor.

Relocated to the south basement, the new kitchen had its own ground-floor ramped access at the western end. The kitchen was very high and fitted with a large skylight for ventilation. There was a complete suite of storage and preparation rooms. The prepared food was despatched to the dining room in a hot-water-jacketed trolley, which ran along narrow-gauge rail tracks for the entire length of the cellars to a dumb waiter at the eastern end. Between the tracks, the woodblock flooring deadened the footfall of the footman as he pushed the trolley towards the dumb waiter. At the eastern end of the dining room, a vertical sliding panel in the ornamental woodwork concealed access to the dumb waiter.

The wine cellar in the east basement was reached separately down stone steps behind an ornately-carved door in the east hall. The brick-built arched bins, dating from 1783, enabled the butler to control and issue the stock directly to staff at the foot of the dumb waiter.

At this period, the 'offices' were in the lower west wing. The ground floor corridor had quarry-tiled floors and the customary long rows of bells and indicators along its ceramic-tiled upper wall. The bells were activated by a hand pull in each reception room and bedroom. The numbered indicators would continue to quiver long after the bells had stopped ringing. On the north side of the corridor was the servants' hall, where most of the servants ate at the long table. To preserve their status, senior servants took their meals separately in the housekeeper's room. A circular stone staircase, with an iron handrail, led to the basement, where the many lower servants' offices such as the boots room were located. Five staircases served the working basement. This was a busy area, particularly during large house parties, when guests would often be accompanied by their own maids, valets and chauffeurs, all needing bed and board.

A gasworks was located near the west end of the lake, to fuel lighting at the Hall when it was restored after the 1866 fire. Early in the 20th century, low power electricity, suitable only for lighting, replaced the gas illumination in the hallways and staircase. At first, this was a 50-volt direct current supply produced by a generator that was belt driven by an early diesel engine. This was housed at Crewe Hall farm so that the oppressive thudding noise of the oil engine would not be intrusive. Very thick copper wires in a trench conducted the current, and continuity of supply was maintained through a bank of large glass accumulator batteries. Although converted to electricity, the light fittings and shades in the east and front halls are original. The pendentive gasoliers that Barry installed in the marble hall had fishtail jets with naked flames until incandescent gas mantles were fitted in the 1880s. Electric cables were routed through these gasoliers when eight reproduction fittings were installed in 1971.

Rogers Field & Co, a specialist firm of civil engineers from London, designed new water supply, drainage, sewage disposal and sanitary arrangements for the Hall in 1896. Their design provided for seven baths, plus two (of lower-grade copper and enamelled iron respectively) for use by servants. Twenty-five lavatories were installed. Hot water from the new boiler system was available in most of the twenty sinks and seven hand basins (two with shampooing fittings). Sewage was discreetly disposed of across the fields about half a mile from the Hall, in the proximity of Weston Road.

There were four sources of water: pumped from the lake by turbine to a reserve tank of 3,000 gallons in the tower; drinking water from a spring at Pinfold pumped by water wheel pumps to the Hall and estate cottages; rainwater piped from the roofs to an underground tank in the courtyard for laundry use, and for the automatic periodic flushing of drainage systems; and an open brickwork reservoir of 28,000 gallons for garden watering and domestic purposes on Philips Hill, fed by a branch of the Englesea Brook, which may have been that installed by Gabriel Smith in 1685.

The Crewes' last head gardener was Bob Spence, a taciturn Scot from Ayton near Berwick, who had served his apprenticeship at the Earl of Mansfield's seat, Scone Palace. After further experience on a Clydeside estate, he was appointed head inside gardener by Lady Crewe in 1912, with responsibility for the walled garden. The many glasshouses played to his skills in producing peaches, nectarines, grapes, melons and tomatoes, as well as the carefully phased seasonal production of vegetables and cut flowers for the house. The raising of fruit and vegetables for the Hall table all the year round was a craft that deployed ingenious technology, including hotbeds, forcing houses and glasshouses. On the north side of the walled kitchen garden there was an underground icehouse for the storage of fish, game, poultry and butter, and for the provision of ice for exotic desserts [48].

The head outside gardener was Mr Whittaker, whom WA Nesfield had introduced to Hungerford Crewe back in 1855. Whittaker and his wife had provided temporary quarters in their cottage for Lord Crewe immediately after the fire of 1866. Perhaps for that reason, the Marquess of Crewe refused to dismiss Whittaker despite the Marchioness' dissatisfaction with his work. A compromise division of responsibilities between the two gardeners evidently satisfied both men and both Crewes. The title of head gardener was bestowed on Mr Spence only when Mr Whittaker finally retired.

There was a general suspicion in the town that Lady Crewe had mixed feelings about both Crewe and Crewe Hall. Though relatively small, Crewe had all the factory chimneys of an industrial town. And even before the First World War, the Hall's High Victorian decoration had become unfashionable, almost risibly so.

Where there's Muck Taken in 1909, this photograph of Crewe Works, the town's largest enterprise, suggests the number of factory chimneys that broke the Crewe skyline during its industrial heyday.

Nonetheless, Lord Crewe took a keen interest in local affairs. Unlike his uncle Hungerford, who had never actively involved himself in the affairs of the new town, Robert readily gave his services when his crowded diary permitted. For example, he chaired such bodies as the Crewe Memorial Hospital board. His presence at local public events was notable, and when hospital fêtes were held in the grounds of Crewe Hall, local people enjoyed the open invitation to view (if strictly from a distance) the splendours of the building.

What did Crewe make of the Crewes? The present author's father Hugh Gladden was born in 1886, one of six children of a railway signalman who migrated from London in 1876. In my father's early days, the Crewes were the uncrowned kings. They were saluted with doffed caps as their carriages progressed through the local villages - but not in the town of Crewe itself, where the proud artisans made their gleaming iron horses that steamed the length of the land, the harbingers of a new prosperity for the toiling masses! There was a healthy distaste for those endowed with the trappings of great, inherited wealth. It was accentuated by their affected way of speech, expensively acquired through the public school system; regarded by them as the norm, but as an irritating affliction by the ordinary folk of the railway town, who spoke their own guttural, polyglot dialect. However, there was always respect for a man's personal achievements whether building railway engines or directing affairs of state. For a peer of proven ability like the Marquess of Crewe, there was great and universal regard.

My uncle remained head gardener at Crewe Hall from 1912 to 1937. In my young days, to speak at the Hall of the Crewes in anything other than tones of hushed reverence was quite unthinkable. They had been paramount in the eyes of their servants and were entirely beyond criticism or reproach. I recall being with my uncle at Madeley Manor in 1944 when the Marquess of Crewe came to visit 'Spence' in his rooms before going on a journey to London. The reason for his call was trivial, but the event quite touching. It was as if two old friends were parting, perhaps for the last time. The Marquess at 86 was almost blind but still an erect, commanding figure, with the sort of charismatic presence that caused everyone in the room to stand as he entered. What passed between them is of no importance, but I have never forgotten the touching simplicity of the event and the demonstration of a relationship between master and servant that amounted to a sort of 'kinship'. But there is the conflicting testimony of Lord Crewe's own grandson, who later wrote of his grandfather's *apparent lack of interest in people, masked though it was by unwavering courtesy*[49].

When Asquith formed a war-time coalition Government with the Conservatives in 1915, the Marquess of Crewe reverted to the Lord Presidency of the Council.

Shortly before, the Prime Minister had told a *confidante* that he ranked Crewe number one in ministerial capacity. (This seems surprisingly harsh on his cabinet colleagues, Lloyd George and Churchill, who only registered joint-fourth on the Asquithian scale [50]. Given their own combative style of leadership, it is doubtful if either would ever have adopted the Crewes' faintly self-deprecating family motto, *Sequor Nec Inferior - Though I follow, I am not inferior.*) Crewe also deputised briefly for the Foreign Secretary in 1915, and as President of the Board of Education in 1916. When Lloyd George supplanted Asquith in 1916, Crewe and most of his fellow Liberals were excluded, or excluded themselves, from the reconstituted coalition Government. Effectively, Crewe's cabinet career was over.

Never inactive for long, he developed existing interests and took on new ones. Many of these were in London, where he was already Lord Lieutenant (and served as such until 1944) but now became Chairman of the County Council for 1917-1918; President of London Territorial Army and Air Force Association; President of the London and Greater London Playing Fields Association; Vice-President of the Royal Veterinary College; and sometime Chairman of the Governing Body of Imperial College of Science and Technology. All this was on top of being Chancellor of Sheffield University and Elder Brother of Trinity House. Nor did Lady Crewe stand idly by: in 1920, she was appointed as a JP for London, one of the first women magistrates in Britain.

Lord Curzon, though the grandest of Tory grandees, had nonetheless been impressed by Crewe's work as a Liberal colleague in Asquith's coalition. As Foreign Secretary, in 1922 he offered Crewe the British Embassy in Paris as 'Ambassador Extraordinary and Plenipotentiary to the French Republic'. Although the Crewes suffered a devastating personal tragedy the same year, when their only son Jack died at the age of eleven, they went to Paris. They remained at the Embassy until 1928. By then 71, Crewe wanted to lead a less active public life, and to pursue his personal interests. In the first eighteen months of his retirement, he wrote a two-volume biography of his father-in-law Lord Rosebery, who had recently died.

In 1931, Crewe returned to Cabinet office for three months as Secretary of State for War in Ramsey MacDonald's 'caretaker' National Government. Five years later, aged 78, he was re-elected Liberal Leader in the House of Lords. A trusted elder statesman, he was of assistance to Stanley Baldwin in the early stages of King Edward VIII's abdication crisis in December 1936.

During and immediately after the first world war, it had become clear that increasing costs and taxation levels would force the break up of many large estates. Land rentals had been falling since the 1870s, due to cheap American grain imports and the subsequent development of refrigerated ships bearing meat from south America and the Antipodes. This began the slide for upper class families whose income largely derived from the land. The declining market had already reduced the rental potential of large country mansions. It has been estimated that between 1917 and 1921, one-quarter of England changed hands [50]. The Crewes were no exception. Even before the war there had been intimations of financial difficulties: on 31 March 1910, Robert Crewe had sold a Romney portrait painting of Lady Milnes to the trans-Atlantic art dealers Duveen Brothers for £28,000. Moreover, the Crewes' public life continued to take them away from the Hall for long periods.

In 1921, almost half of the Crewes' Madeley estate was sold by auction at the Crewe Arms Hotel. On average, it fetched £40.0s.0d. per acre. Lord Crewe retained only the Regency manor house and some minor holdings, and the following year, he decided to close Crewe Hall. The furniture and contents were sheeted over while efforts were made to dispose of the property. Carriages and motors lingered unused in the coach houses on the lower floor of the west wing of the stables. The horse-drawn, hand-pumped fire engine, with a horizontal bar on either side, and festoons of leather buckets and copper-riveted leather hose pipe - standard country house issue - remained unused and unuseable without two teams of men to operate it. A single sturdy beast of sedate habits spent his days where 27 horses had once been stabled. Twice a week, he would be harnessed to a trap or a slightly heavier vehicle called a 'shandry' and sent with his keeper, the benevolent Aaron Coppenhall, to Crewe to fetch and carry for the gardens.

For nearly fourteen years, the place had the placid atmosphere of benign neglect. From 1922 to 1939, a caretaker lived in rooms at the north-eastern corner of the stables courtyard. With blinds drawn over most of the Hall's windows, and the grounds overgrown, the place seemed lifeless. Now sadly tarnished, the golden gates on Weston Road were closed permanently. An aerial photograph taken in 1930 captured Crewe Hall in the sleepiest phase of its history.

At first, a team of about six gardeners continued to grow garden produce. The gardens, with their extensive glasshouses, and distinctive boxes stencilled 'Crewe Hall Gardens', had a splendid reputation for quality. There was steady demand from local outlets for the quality produce, until its quality prices could no longer survive the depression of the 1930s. The hard truth was that the head gardener Bob Spence was more of a plantsman than a market garden manager.

During this period, Crewe churches were still allowed to hold their annual Sunday school treats in Crewe Hall park. In the summertime, groups of school children, each equipped with a personal mug tied around the neck with string, travelled to the Hall by horse-drawn wagonette to enjoy an hour or two of organised games in the extensive parkland.

In protracted negotiations with Cheshire County Council, Lord Crewe offered the Hall and 25 acres without charge (except for a payment of £500 for the land) as new headquarters. Instead, the County Council decided to build a new County Hall in Chester.

The estate was finally sold to the Duchy of Lancaster (in effect, the King). On 14 March 1936, 'The Times' reported the sale of the *estate ...of 4,380 acres with Hall, Home Farm, 50 farms, many small holdings and fully 100 cottages. Lord Crewe retained a small village area surrounding the church at Barthomley...*

Lord Crewe explained the sale to his tenants: *We have not been in residence at Crewe Hall for many years, and my eldest daughter and her son, to whom the*

Enchanted Castle Crewe Hall photographed from the air c. 1930, eight years after the family home was closed down and when the grounds were increasingly overgrown.

68

property will pass, will not find it possible to live there…It is some eight hundred years since there was first a Crewe of Crewe; and we observe tradition by retaining the immediate village surroundings of the Church and churchyard at Barthomley, where so many generations of our forbears rest..I am happy to think that by becoming tenants of His Majesty the King the occupants of holdings are merely exchanging an ownership which I hope has been liberal and sympathetic for another conducted on similar lines; and I am glad to know that Mr W. McCracken, who is the friend of everybody on the estate, will continue to live at Englesea House, and that his advice will be available to all who need it during the period of transition…Changes such as this can never be welcome; but it is a consolation to be able to say goodbye to the tenants of farms, the small-holders and the cottagers on these properties and to wish them well, with confidence that the change is not one which will be hurtful to them or their homes. Caring and paternalistic to the end, Lord Crewe's behaviour contrasted with that of the Earl of Lonsdale who, in similar financial straits, had two months earlier closed down his vast Cumberland pile without a word of appreciation or regret to its staff.

All the movable items were taken from Crewe Hall, and many were sold. In 1932, the Crewes had moved to West Horsley Place, near Leatherhead in Surrey. At the beginning of the Second World War, they were persuaded on medical advice to return to Madeley Manor, which had been unoccupied for some years. The ever-faithful Bob Spence left Crewe Hall to provide them with a regular supply of homegrown vegetables worked from the much smaller garden at Madeley. Later in the War, the Crewes moved to the Lady Crewe's childhood home at Mentmore.

Robert Crewe died on 20 June 1945 at West Horsley Place, full of years and honours: the first and last Marquess of Crewe in the County Palatine of Chester, Earl of Madeley in the County of Staffordshire, and Baron Houghton of Great Houghton in the West Riding of the County of York; Knight of the Most Noble Order of the Garter; Royal Victorian Chain; Grand Cross of the Legion of Honour of France; Order (First Class) of the White Eagle of Serbia; Honorary Doctor of Law of the Universities of Cambridge, Leeds, and Liverpool; Honorary Doctor of Civil Law of the Universities of Durham and Oxford... His peerages died with him. He was himself an only son, and both of his own boys died before they grew up. There was no remainder that allowed his title - as it had allowed those of canny contemporaries like Lords Curzon and Rhondda - to pass through the female line.

In the family tradition, Lord Crewe was buried at Barthomley. In 1925-26, he had had the church restored as a memorial to his two dead sons. Inside, a handsome white marble sculpture by Sir Joseph Edgar Boehm RA (1834-1890) commemorates the Marquess's long-dead first wife, Sybil. His Garter standard, which hung during his lifetime in the choir of St. George's Chapel at Windsor Castle, now decorates the chancel. Outside, the Crewe graves - those of Hungerford Crewe, and the Marquess, his first wife (his second wife survived until 1967), and his young son, Richard - are on the south side of the churchyard.

Only a simple chain separates their last resting places from those of their tenants.

Chapter 8

WAR AND PEACE

Let Us Face the Future [52]

Whatever Lord Crewe's hopes had been, change was inevitable after the sale of Crewe Hall in 1936, not least because of the deterioration in international affairs.

This was not immediately apparent. The agent, Mr W McCracken, continued to rule the estates as a benevolent despot from Englesea House, the Crewe agent's traditional perquisite on the Alsager road just beyond the boundary of the park. Colonel Deneys followed after McCracken's death. The Crewe estate office, which also dealt with the affairs of the smaller residual estate at Madeley, was transferred to Imperial Chambers in Prince Albert Street in Crewe. The Colonel's son, Captain Deneys, followed him in the post in the 1950s.

Shortly after the Duchy of Lancaster purchased the Hall, Crewe borough council decided to build an aerodrome near the railway station. At the time, airports were conceived on a much smaller scale than today, and 343 acres at Crewe Gates Farm was considered adequate. Purchase of the land for £45,000 was agreed in August 1937. The Council borrowed £32,000 from the Ministry of Health, and the remaining £13,000 from Cheshire County Council [53]. In the event, the land was never used as an airfield, but proved to have been a very sound investment when the council developed the Weston Road industrial estate in the early 1960s.

The Duchy of Lancaster had no immediate use for the Hall itself, although Lord Crewe retained the gardens after the sale, and they were worked commercially for a time. By the start of the second world war, seventeen years of neglect since 1922 had stored up problems of dry rot and deathwatch beetle with which post-War tenants would have to deal. However, the war helped to preserve Crewe Hall by creating a use for it. In 1939, the War Office leased the Hall from the Duchy. Successive waves of British, American and Allied troops were based there. On the instruction of the War Office, JT Gresty & Sons of Willaston constructed 79 numbered brick huts on the former Nesfield gardens on the east front, as close to the Hall as they could conveniently could. Others were attached to the east side of the stables, and in its courtyard; alongside the front steps of the Hall; and across the southwest front lawn. They were erected in herring-bone formation along both sides of the main drive, and scattered liberally over the former approaches to the grove and woodland walks at the eastern end of the 'pleasure gardens'.

71

Expediency not aesthetics dominated the construction of a wartime army camp, and no control was exercised over where or how the buildings were erected. Many of the smaller huts were demolished after the War, but the larger buildings went on to form the basis for Calmic's first factory in 1946.

After use as a training camp, Crewe Hall became a repatriation camp for troops returning from Dunkirk in 1940. The Hall itself was used as an administration block and as officer's quarters. In the spring of 1943, the marble hall was furnished with a plotting table to become the gun operations room co-ordinating local air and ground defences in the north Midlands and north Wales.

Another access road was laid from the main drive to the stable courtyard, for use by the Transport Section, skirting the western perimeter of the camp. Site roads were put down as required, the main carriage drive was reopened. Left open permanently, the golden gates were eventually embedded in successive layers of macadam. Their condition became so dilapidated and dangerous that they had to be dismantled completely in 1950. When American troops occupied and extended the camp, the sewage works had to be upgraded, and the benefits of a modern disposal system proved useful to Crewe Hall's industrial tenants after the war.

Exposed carvings and decorations in the Hall were carefully dismantled, or covered with protective wire mesh frames. Staircase treads and flooring suffered the effect of hobnail boots, but military tenants were fairly responsible custodians. Inside, the decoration looked neglected by the end of the War, but the fabric of the building itself remained reasonably sound. Outside, the dam and culvert that retained the waters of the stream gave way in 1943 and the Repton lake drained away to the Irish Sea, via the Weaver and the Mersey. Some of the statuary suffered from the vagaries of military occupation. Two large stone lions were taken from their pedestals flanking the terrace on the north front, and placed on each side of the main entrance front steps.

Late in 1943, the site became Camp 191, an Oflag prison for approximately 2,000 German army officers. During this time, it was occupied by the small British army garrison that guarded the prisoners. Both officers and men used the Hall for living and working accommodation, and Hungerford Crewe's old bedroom served as the sergeants' mess [54].

The prisoners' offer to reinstate the dam was turned down as likely to raise the morale of those volunteering. A substantial barbed wire perimeter fence was erected around the camp, with elevated guard towers equipped with machine guns. An enclosed area on the south-east lawn was known as the cage, where prisoners were paraded for interminable roll calls in all weathers. There was a self-imposed, daily routine of sports, classes and lectures. The prisoners levelled some ground for use as a 'sportsplatz' for their own organised games; it later became a tennis court for Calmic sports club members. They ran their own symphony orchestra and theatre company in what was termed the 'Schlosstheater'. Photographs of their homemade stage sets show considerable ingenuity and improvisation.

Although the POWs endured much hardship in captivity, with cold winters and short rations, conditions for the Wehrmacht at Camp 191 were considered to be less severe than those at other British prison camps. Along with about one third of all prisoners of war in Britain, some Crewe Hall POWs worked on the land. Nonetheless, other prisoners devised a well-planned escape scheme, and extensive tunnelling over many months nearly resulted in a successful breakout. However, on 14 March 1945, British army field security personnel discovered the tunnels under the huts, and the attempt was foiled [55].

After the second world war, repatriation of the 402,200 German POWs in Britain was not completed until July 1948. Camp 191 closed in April 1947. Evidence at Crewe Hall of the German occupation are the autographs etched in the lead flashing above the main staircase skylight, and a rudimentary sundial carved on the balustrade wall on the west side of the main gateway.

The War Office surrendered its lease of the Hall. There were strong rumours, then and later, that the building would become the projected University College of North Staffordshire, but Keele Hall triumphed. The Duchy of Lancaster leased the Hall and 25 acres of ground to Calmic Ltd. Calmic had been incorporated in February 1932 by a Warrington solicitor, Frank Dunkerley, and his cousin, Harold Ward. Initially, the company operated a toilet deodorisation service from Liverpool. Bombed out in 1942, Calmic moved to Westhoughton, near Bolton. Having diversified into factoring and the elementary manufacture of industrial medical products, by early 1946 the firm needed more space for their activities, and the Duchy sold them the War Office buildings at Crewe as a useful start for the new factory. Although Calmic moved in during the spring of 1947, their liaison officer Hugh Mallinson and his wife had been living in temporary accommodation over the stables since the previous November, while the Hall was still a prison camp. This liaison had many benefits, including employment of the site foreman who had previously worked for the army garrison engineer.

As soon as the POW camp closed, Calmic Limited moved in eight essential workers and their families. Each family was provided with a complete suite of rooms. The essential personnel occupying rooms at Crewe Hall included Hugh Mallinson and Cyril Longworth, both of whom late became directors of Calmic Limited. Apocryphally, when the company chairman was looking for a suitable

73

office, he was advised to find the room that had served as the sergeants' mess, as this was likely to have been the best accommodation in the building.

The Hall required considerable redecoration and rewiring to make the rooms habitable as offices. The larger rooms served as open plan offices. During the first winter of 1947-48, they were heated at great inefficiency and even greater expense by coal fires in the enormous old-fashioned grates. The original 1840 heating system was tried, but did little more than fill the Hall with sulphurous fumes. A coal-fired central heating system was installed during the summer of 1947, requiring installation of a boiler in the old kitchen and construction of a new chimney up the inside of the well of the West wing. At about this time, the Duchy shortened the Hall's tall octagonal chimneys to make them safe.

To begin with, Calmic employed fewer than 100 staff, but with the inception of the National Health Service in 1948, they started to expand their modest range of prescribable medical and veterinary products, and the business expanded substantially. Progressively greater use was made of the rooms in the Hall, and alterations of existing accommodation were agreed with the Duchy of Lancaster. By inserting a first floor into the lofty billiards room with its upper gallery, and partitioning the resultant area, the floor space was almost doubled.

During the 1950s, the major rooms in the Hall received the attention of an enthusiastic decorating team who were very sympathetic to the need for restoration to the Barry standard of eighty years before. The original gold leaf was cleaned up on the most ornate strapwork ceilings in the library and the drawing room, and test scrapings taken of the original colouring before painstaking restoration was begun.

Some rooms were obvious choices for specific functions. The butler's pantry became the cashier's office, with the plate closet serving as strongroom. A men's lavatory was created in the unused lobby space that, in pre-tower days, had been the rosebud bedroom. The Victorian Chubb safe was left *in situ* but fitted with a baize-lined jewellery tray for the storage of company minute books and registers from 1950 to 1970. The servants' bedrooms in the attics were converted to offices in the late 1960s, leading to construction of an external fire escape on the east elevation of the Hall to meet fire safety regulations.

Development of the factory site on the east side of Crewe Hall demanded extended services, and a central oil-fired boiler was installed inside the complex to serve the whole site including the Hall. Modification of the Hall continued. When all useable rooms had been put into service, a modern office extension was constructed in 1965 next to, and connecting with, the west wing. This required demolition of one of the two Barry summerhouses on the North front. The decorative animals were brought to the front entrance of the Hall, where they still grace the balustrade wall in place of the original stone balls.

The grounds of the Hall required considerable preparation before the spacious lawns could be reinstated. The army had used the lawned area south-east of the Hall for a parade ground and a prison cage. This needed to be ploughed and planted with a potato crop before grass seed could be sown.

By 1966, 772 staff were employed at Crewe Hall. Calmic had diversified into engineering and printing, and opened branches in many parts of the world. In that year, The Wellcome Foundation acquired Calmic Limited from its original owners and established its UK Region Headquarters at Crewe Hall, and in 1970 they acquired a 99 year lease from the Duchy of Lancaster. In 1974, the company embarked on the largest restoration of the building since 1870. It lasted four years. The exterior was sand blasted and cleaned; much of the friable red sandstone was replaced with Hollington sandstone of a more durable type; brickwork was comprehensively repaired; lead roofing and guttering was replaced; and chimneys were reduced and capped. Inside the Hall, every room, large or small, was revitalised; and the building was completely rewired.

Royal Visit (II) HM Queen Elizabeth II visits the Wellcome Foundation.

The stables, earlier used as workshop accommodation, were adapted to serve as offices and laboratories. The old wooden sliding doors of the coach houses were converted into windows, fitted into the existing stone arched doorways; and the rotting upper floors were completely replaced.

But changes were afoot. In 1994, the Duchy of Lancaster sold the Crewe Hall site to St Modwen Properties. In 1995, Wellcome amalgamated with another pharmaceutical giant, Glaxo, and later that year Glaxo-Wellcome left the Hall. Once again, the property stood empty until St Modwen sold it on to Phillip Humphreys for conversion to a hotel. The Hall reopened as an hotel the same year, and was sold in 2003 to Marston Hotels, and subsequently to the QHotels group. Set in eight acres of parkland, it has 117 bedrooms, including 25 located in the old building; a restaurant and a brasserie; conference facilities; a health club with gym, spa, swimming pool and tennis courts. Nonetheless, a flavour lingers of the old days. The Duchy of Lancaster still owns a large area of the estate, and manages it as dairy farms and woodland, with some commercial development near Crewe and at Crewe Hall Farm.

Heirs and Successors (I) The Marquess of Crewe's journalist grandson Quentin Crewe.

Nor did the Crewes vanish into total obscurity when the Marquess of Crewe sold Crewe Hall. Lady Mary, Crewe's surviving child by his second marriage, became the first wife of the Duke of Roxburghe and (in the autumn of 2011) lives on in her 97th year. Of Lord Crewe's three daughters by his first marriage, Lady Annabel married the Hon Arthur O'Neill. One of their grandchildren is the historian and broadcaster Bamber Gascoigne. Their son Terence, later Lord O'Neill of the Maine, was Prime Minister of Northern Ireland from 1963 to 1969 - perhaps not the form of Irish Home Rule that his grandfather Crewe had had in mind seventy years earlier. In November 1914, Arthur O'Neill was the first MP to be killed in action, and in 1922 his widow married Hugh Dodds. When Lord Crewe died, the Dodds changed their name by deed poll to Crewe. An undergraduate friend of their son, Quentin, joked *How odd of Dodds/To choose the Crewes*, a sly reference to their Rothschild ancestry and Ewer's *How odd of God/To choose the Jews*. Thus re-christened, Quentin Crewe became a well-known author and journalist.

Lady Annabel's sister Celia married a Yorkshire baronet, Sir Clive Coates. Their grandson, Professor Sir Anthony Milnes Coates, occupies the chair of medical microbiology at St George's Medical School in the University of London. Lady Celia's twin sister Cynthia married the Hon George Colville, and was for many years a member of HM Queen Mary's household. Her son Jock, later Sir John Colville, served as private secretary to three successive Prime Ministers (Chamberlain, Churchill, Attlee), and later to HRH Princess Elizabeth, now HM The Queen.

Heirs and Successors (II) The Marquess of Crewe's broadcaster-historian great grandson Bamber Gascoigne.

Though I follow, I am not inferior.

APPENDIX

Owners of Crewe Hall 1608-1936

The following members of the Crewe family were **owners** of Crewe Hall:

Sir Ranulphe Crewe 1558-1646, who bought the Crewe estate 1608; who was knighted 1614; who built Crewe Hall 1615-1636; and who was succeeded by his son:

Sir Clippesby Crewe 1599-1649, who was succeeded by his son:

John Crewe 1626-1684, who was succeeded by his daughter:

Ann Crewe-Offley 1649-1711, who was succeeded by her son:

John Crewe 1681-1749, who changed his surname from Crewe-Offley to Crewe 1708, and was succeeded by his son:

John Crewe 1707-1752, who was succeeded by his son:

John Crewe, first Baron Crewe 1742-1829, who was raised to the peerage as Baron Crewe 1806, and was succeeded in that title by his son:

John Crewe, second Baron Crewe 1772-1835, who did not inherit the Crewe estate, which was bequeathed to:

Hungerford Crewe, third Baron Crewe 1812-1894, who inherited the estate from his grandfather, the first Baron Crewe, and who was succeeded by his sister's son:

Robert Offley Ashburton Crewe-Milnes, first Marquis of Crewe 1858-1945, who changed his surname from Milnes to Crewe-Milnes 1894; was raised in the peerage from second Baron Houghton to Earl of Crewe 1895; was further elevated to Marquis of Crewe and Earl of Madeley 1911; and sold Crewe Hall to the Duchy of Lancaster 1936.

Acknowledgements

Many people and organisations supported the compilation of this book. Particular thanks are due to The Wellcome Foundation; the County Archivist and staff of the Cheshire Record Office; the Principal Librarian and staff of the Crewe Public Library; the Surveyor and staff of the Duchy of Lancaster at Crewe; Michael Allen of Enfield; S Astley of the Victoria and Albert Museum; the late Quentin Crewe; David Gladden, of Crewe; G Dodd of Nantwich; K Goodway and R Speake of Keele University; EW Lighton of Crewe; J Piggott of Dulwich College; and B Rizzo of City College, New York

BIBLIOGRAPHY AND FURTHER READING

Primary sources were restricted to public papers at Crewe Public Library and to Crewe family papers at the Cheshire County Record Office at Chester. Members of the Crewe family have reclaimed from the latter collection certain material that may become available again in future years. Fortunately, the Marquess of Crewe was a keen family historian who compiled useful notes around 1920.

Ashley, Maurice [Sir] *England in the Seventeenth Century* Penguin, 1952

Bostock, AJ *The Chivalry of Cheshire* Morten, Manchester, 1980

Builder, The Journal for 19 June 1869

Carter, George; Goode, Patrick; and Laurie, Kedrun *Humphry Repton, Landscape Gardener, 1752-1818* London, 1983

Chaloner, WH *The Social and Economic Development of Crewe 1780-1923* Manchester University Press, 1950

Colville, Cynthia [Lady] *Crowded Life* Evans, London, 1963

Colville, J *The Fringes of Power* London, 1985

Colvin, J *Biographical Dictionary of British Architects, 1600-1840* Murray, London, 1978

Cullen, PW and Horden, R *Castles of Cheshire* C & H Publishers, 1986

Davies, Jennifer *The Victorian Kitchen Garden* BBC Books, London, 1987

Figueirado P de and Treuherz J *Cheshire Country Houses* Phillimore, Chichester, 1988

Fisher, GW *Annals of Shrewsbury School* 1899

Fraser, Antonia *King James VI of Scotland, I of England.* Weidenfeld and Nicolson, London, 1974

Galbraith, Georgina (Editor) *The Journal of the Rev William Bagshaw Stevens* Clarendon Press, Oxford, 1965

Gentleman's Magazine, The London, March 1866

Girouard, Mark *Life in the English Country House* Yale University Press, New Haven and London, 1978

Girouard, Mark *The Victorian Country House* Yale University Press, Newhaven and London, 1979

Gladden, Walter *Cheshire Folk* Heath Cranton Ltd, London, 1932

Gunnis, Rupert *Dictionary of British Sculptors 1660-1851* The Abbey Library, London, 1951

Hall, James *A History of Nantwich* Nantwich, 1883

Harris, John *The Artist and the Country House* Sotheby Parke Benet, London, 1979

Hinchliffe, the Rev Edward *Barthomley* Longman, Brown, Green and Longman, London, 1856

Hodson, J Howard *Cheshire, 1660-1780: Restoration to Industrial Revolution* Cheshire Community Council, 1978

Jervis, Simon *Penguin Dictionary of Design and Designers*

Kennedy, J *Madeley. A History of a Staffordshire Parish* Keele University, 1970

King, Daniel *The Vale Royal of England* Chester, 1656

Kochan, Miriam *Prisoners of England* Macmillan Press, London, 1980

Latham, Robert and Mathews, William. (Editors) *The Diary of Samuel Pepys.* Vols.II.and X Bell and Hyman, London, 1983

Marks, H. Stacey *Pen and Pencil Sketches* London, 1894

Moss, Fletcher *The Fifth Book of Pilgrimages to Old Homes* Didsbury, 1910

Mowl, T and Earnshaw, B *Trumpet at a Distant Gate: The Lodge as Prelude to the Country House* Waterstone, London, 1985

Ormerod, Dr. George *History of Cheshire:* Vol.III 2nd edition, London, 1882

Pevsner, Nikolaus and Hubbard, Edward *The Buildings of England:- Cheshire* Penguin, London, 1971

Phillimore. *Domesday Cheshire* Chichester, 1978

Pine, LG *The New Extinct Peerage, 1844-1971* London, 1972

Pope-Hennessy, James *Lord Crewe 1858-1945: The Likeness of a Liberal* Constable, London, 1955

Richards, Raymond *Old Cheshire Churches* Batsford London, 1947

Scard, Geoffrey *Squire and Tenant: Rural Life in Cheshire 1760-1900* Cheshire Community Council, 1981

Stone, Lawrence *The Crisis of the Aristocracy 1558-1641* Oxford University Press, 1965

Stroud, Dorothy *Capability Brown* Faber and Faber, London, 1975

Stroud, Dorothy *Humphry Repton* , Country Life, 1962

Summerson, John *Architecture in Great Britain 1530-1830* Pelican History of Art, London, 1969

Sylvester, Dorothy *A History of Cheshire* Phillimore, Chichester, 1980

Young, Peter [Brigadier] and Emberton, Wilfred *Sieges of the Great Civil War* Bell and Hyman, London, 1978

Other written or illustrated references not listed elsewhere:

Burke JB *Visitation of Seats: Volume 1, 9* 1852

Country Life 29 March 1902, 3 May 1913

Hall, SC *Baronial Halls: volume 1* 1848

Latham, C *In English Homes: volume 1* 1904

Nash, J *Mansions of England:* Volumes I,II 1839, 1849.

Richardson, CJ *Old English Mansions: Volumes I, II* 1841, 1842

Twycross, E *Mansions of England and Wales Volume II* 1850

The following pictures help to explain developments in the building
  of Crewe

c.1655 drawing by Wenceslaus Hollar reproduced in *'The Vale Royal of England'*
by Daniel King of Chester, 1656. The original engraving of this drawing is in the
private collection of Her Majesty the Queen

c.1710 painting by an unknown artist. In a private collection. Photograph by
Courtesy of the Courtauld Institute of Art

1742 drawing by William Yoxall reproduced in *'Magna Brittannia'* by D. & S.
Lysons. 1810

1818 drawing by J.P. Neale reproduced in *'Views of Seats'* by the artist

1851 drawing by Augustus Butler reproduced in *'Selections from Views of
Mansions'* by J. Bartlett. 1870

Photographs of Crewe Hall presented to Hungerford, Third Lord Crewe by
W. Cubitt & Company London

REFERENCES

CPL   Crewe Public Library
CRO   Cheshire Record Office
HBMC Historic Buildings and Monuments Commission

1   Gilbert, William Schwenck, [Sir] from *Iolanthe*, 1882

2   *Burke's Peerage, Baronetage and Knightage* 107th edition, 2003

3   Jenkins, Simon *England's Thousand Best Houses* Allen Lane, 2003

4   Phillimore *Domesday Cheshire* Colchester, 1978

5   Ormerod, George *A History of Cheshire* London, 1882

6   CRO, DCR/27/4 The Will of Sir Ranulphe Crewe

7   King, D   *The Vale Royal of England*   Chester, 1656

8   Hinchliffe, E *Barthomley* London, 1856

9   Hall, J *A History of Nantwich* Nantwich, 1883

10   Ashley, Maurice [Sir] *England in the Seventeenth Century* Penguin, 1952

11   Stone, L   *The Crisis of the Aristocracy 1558 to 1641* Oxford, 1965

12   CRO, DCR/3687/6 Synopsis of Crewe Family history written by the Marquess of Crewe

13   Hubbard, Edward   Notes prepared as co-author of *Buildings of England: Cheshire* for the Manchester Victorian Society in the mid 1960s

14   Mowl, T and Earnshaw, B
     Trumpet at a Distant Gate: Trumpet at a Distant Gate: The Lodge as Prelude to the Country House London, 1985

15   Girouard, M   *Life in the English Country House* New Haven and London, 1978

16   Sylvester, D   *A History of Cheshire* Colchester, 1980

17   Kennedy, J *Madeley: A History of a Staffordshire Parish* Keele, 1970

18   CRO, DCR/26/4c/28 'Artikelles ffor ye Waterworkes at Crewe': Agreement between John Crewe Offley and Gabriel Smith, 7 January 1688

19   CRO, DCR/28/21 Inventory of Goods of John Offley

20   Harris, J *The Artist and the Country House* London, 1979

21   Hodson, JH *Cheshire 1660-1780: Restoration to Industrial Revolution*
      Chester, 1978

22   CRO, DCR/55A Letter of 3 April 1724 from William Rawlins

23   Scard, G *Squire and Tenant : Rural Life in Cheshire 1760-1900*
      Chester, 1981

24   Allen, Michael *Dickens Quarterly* US publication, December 1988

25   Lewis, WS *A Guide to the Life of Horace Walpole 1717-1797* New
      Haven and London, 1973

26   Neale, JP *Views of Seats: Volume 1* London, 1818

27   CRO, DCR/15/2: Alterations to Crewe Hall 1772-1804

28   Goodway, K *Historic Parks and Gardens in the North West* Adlington
      Hall Symposium, 1985

29   Historic Manuscripts Commission *Tours of Earl of Verulam* , 1906

30   CRO, DCR/58/1 Lord Crewe's Cheshire Estates 1801-64

31   Duchy of Lancaster Crewe Office Archives Survey by Samuel Wyatt
      of 'The Lordship of Crewe and surrounding lands' 1767

32   The Burney Letters Berg Collection, New York Public Library

33   Galbraith, G (editor) *The Journal of the Rev. William Bagshaw Stevens*
      Oxford, 1965

34   Colville, C [Lady] *Crowded Life* London, 1963

35   CRO, DCR/58/10 The Will of John, First Lord Crewe

36   CRO, DCR/58/1 Lord Crewe's Cheshire Estates, 1801-64

37   CRO, DCR/55A/32 Letters of Mrs Offley, 1823-49

38   Crewe Public Library Archives 'Cash Book 1844-7 of Mr EH Martin'

39   Chaloner, WH *The Social and Economic Development of Crewe 1780-
      1923* Manchester University Press, 1950.

40   CRO, DCR/38/2/2 Agreement for sale of land to North Staffordshire
      Railway Company 14 January 1861 and Indenture of 29 October 1862

41   Cheshire RO, DCR/15/2 Correspondence and Reports to Lord Crewe
      from WA Nesfield re Landscaping 1842-66

42   CRO, DCR/3687/4 Letter from Hungerford Third Lord Crewe re
      Stables

43   CRO, DCR/3687/8 Papers re Advowson of Astbury

44   Arley Hall Collection 'The Latham Letters': letters to to Rowland Egerton Warburton

45   Colvin, HM *Biographical Dictionary of British Architects 1600 to 1840* London, 1978

46   Burgess, FD *By Royal Command: The Story of Fodens Motor Works Band* (Elworth, 1977) 11

47   Archives of the Duchy of Lancaster at Englesea House, Crewe Housekeeper's Inventory 1876-90

48   Davies, J *The Victorian Kitchen Garden* London, 1987

49   Colville, J *The Fringes of Power* London, 1985

50   Brock, M and E (editors)

      HH Asquith: Letters to Venetia Stanley Oxford 1982

51   Littlejohn, David *The Fate of the English Country House* Oxford University Press, 1997

52   Title of Labour Party manifesto 1945

53   *Crewe Chronicle* reports of Crewe Borough Council proceedings of 1 January and 1 February 1938

54   Kochan, M *Prisoners of England* London, 1980

55   *Tabloid* (Wellcome plc house journal) March 1985

56   Carroll, Lewis *Through the Looking Glass and What Alice Found There* London, 1871

57   Kennan, GF, American historian, on 20th century British social history quoted by Cooke, Alistair on BBC Radio's *Letter from America*